ROCKHOUNDING
FOR BEGINNERS

ADVANCED PACK

All You Need To Know To Pass From Beginner
To Advanced. Learn How To Find, Clean,
Cut And Polish All Types Of Rocks

ROGER BROWN

HOW CAN YOU FOLLOW ROGER?

JOIN IN MY PRIVATE FB GROUP

FOLLOW MY FB PAGE

TABLE OF CONTENTS

INTRODUCTION

If you have this book in your hands, it is because you have been interested in learning about rockhounding; start looking for stones in different ways, this activity at first glance looks simple, go, dig the earth and take out rocks to get them beautiful in a showcase at home or sell them, but, like everything exciting, it has its degree of difficulty.

Do not be scared or run because, if you follow the advice based on the experience I have prepared in this book, it will be very easy to start collecting rocks, have the right tools, know the space in which you are going to work, and having the indications and rules for the profession.

I have decided to prepare the book going from the basics, which is deciphering what rockhounding is, knowing how rocks are identified, how to do it, the passion so entertaining it is, reasons for you to start in this world, uses of rocks and the first tips for you to take steps in the collection.

Then, I will tell you about the history of rockhounding, related stories, what happened after the Civil War, and the need for some that led them to dig the earth to find something of value.

You cannot be left out of the section of laws and regulations that have to be taken into account because I teach you according to the validity where and where not to look for rocks, those limited places, and where you cannot even appear with a pick or a chisel.

Before you go out to look for rocks, you will learn how to know the locations thanks to a website full of big data that will be your right hand in this whole adventure, as well as other applications that will be as useful as the hammer or the pickaxe to dig.

In the next chapter, I talk about clothes, with advice from experience that you will not find anywhere else; if you follow them, the journey will be enjoyable, and surely no setbacks will appear.

Then, I will tell you about the rocks, what they are, and the types, and then address the ones that interest us, gems, minerals, geodes, etc. I separated them in such a way that you understand them well and know how to learn to differentiate them.

If you have doubts about identifying the rocks, I will leave you a chapter where I will teach you how to do it. You will see how you can have your rocks classified without error.

Surely the tips on finding rocks will be very helpful, so you will not get frustrated when digging in the earth without luck.

Then, to avoid missing a detail, I teach you how to clean the rocks correctly without damaging or hurting your hands; the same applies to the chapter where I teach you how to cut and polish them.

This book is a bible, where you will go from beginner to advance in rockhounding.

CHAPTER #1
LET'S START LEARNING WHAT ROCKHOUNDING IS

Rockhounding, also known as amateur geology, is the recreational study and collecting of gems, rocks, minerals, and fossils from the natural environment.

Minerals of solid non-organic substances with specific chemical compositions and crystal structures are naturally found in pure form. Gemstones are precious or semi-precious minerals that can be cut and polished. Gold is not a gem or a mineral but a chemical element.

A rock chase is where people gather or collect rocks, minerals, gems, and fossils from various places. Many people call it rock hunting; others might call it amateur geology or rock and mineral gathering. It is usually always considered a hobby.

Rockhound is a term used to describe a person whose hobby is collecting rocks and minerals. Being a rock hound would mean that someone would have a certain collection of rocks and minerals. It may seem strange to some, but many will realize how addictive it can be when you first ride it.

Before you take the plunge to try this hobby as a beginner, you might want to understand what it takes to be a rock hound. It's important to be prepared and understand a little bit about what you're doing and what to expect. This section will give you more details on how to start a beginner's rock hunting trip and how to prepare.

You'll want to do some research before you start:

- What are the best places to go looking for rocks where you live?
- Are the rocks available where you live?
- How do I get to this site?

For example, looking for rocks such as agate and jasper that can be polished on a rotating machine along the coast of Tillamook is common. Others look for igneous rocks (volcanic rocks) with air bubbles into which minerals have penetrated and crystallized.

Still, others are looking for fossils. I like to throw my stones on shiny surfaces, so I mainly look for agate and jasper.

How Are Rocks Detected?

Although later I will explain it to you and you will learn it throughout the pages, I advance a little on what you should take into account to detect rocks.

Everyone in my house looks for rocks differently. I compare it to coloring in a coloring book: some of us outline first, then we color; others color or "doodle" in all directions; and still others fill with color with parallel, straight and intentional lines so as not to lose anything.

Some like the doodle method. These people say the lines existed as "suggestions." I like to color and look for rocks in parallel straight lines, from the top line of the bedrock to the low tide line and vice versa.

What about the segmentation method? Think of bedrock as a grid. There are perhaps six sections, and you will read each carefully.

Some have focused their searches on wavy lines, which are wet and glow with water droplets on rocks, making them easier to spot.

Take the time to be curious. Think about what might be hidden or just below the surface. You can dig for treasure!

What Is the Best Time to Spot Rocks?

It all depends on where you are and the weather; for example, Oregon's main agate hunting season is usually between October and April, when large storms erode the levees and drag the sand, exposing the rocks.

You'll want to plan to visit the beach at low tide. As noted by M. J. Grover in his book Onyx Hunting on the Oregon Coast, "the protruding tides stirred the bedrock, bringing sand into the sea, exposing the bedrock below."

How to Identify Rocks

Depending on the area, you can find, for example, a variety of agates, including carnelian agate, milk agate (also known as white agate or moonstone agate), banded agate, defense agate, cloud agate, and moss agate.

What they have in common is that agate is translucent. It means that when you hold them, you can see the light passing through them.

To me, beautiful jasper is as precious as agate! Jasper is an opaque stone with bold colors and impurities that give it its vivid reds, greens, yellows, and browns. You can identify jasper by its soft texture and bright color.

The most famous (and highest) site in Chaffee County is Mount Antero, where a variety of semi-precious stones have been found, including aquamarine and smoky quartz. You must make sure to avoid remnants.

In addition, some sites still have a claims system. Claims are usually marked with pillars or stelae and must be respected. Occasionally, rock hunting clubs provide members with group-specific statements.

If you are interested in gems and want to find them, how you do it:

A good number of recreational rock prospectors want to collect on the surface. Official digging sites (where you usually pay) can be a good source of more common gems, and there are often places to help you search. However, you're unlikely to find anything strange or particularly cool there.

The first task is to learn how to identify gems accurately. The Coors Museum of Minerals at the Denver Museum of Nature and Science, or the Geology Museum at the Colorado School of Mines in Golden, Colorado, is worth a visit. The former is easy to navigate if you're flying to Denver. Both sites have extensive collections, boasting great examples of minerals found in the state, so you can identify any gems you find. You can also get a gem recognition app for your mobile or be a classic and buy a book.

Learning to find gems can be a big challenge. For those starting, it's best to find a hunting hound club with a planned trip, where you can hunt with more experienced people who can help you train your eyesight and recognize your findings.

What should I do after I find the gem? If you're serious, consider buying a gemstone display case or organizer: keep gems in a jewelry bag or gem jar.

You can have a merchant evaluate gems, and if you find something exceptionally valuable, you might consider selling them. However, most people collect gems for display.

You can even go to a rock and gem show to showcase your collection to the public.

Looking for Rocks Is a Great Passion That Entertains

Anyone who has camped in the desert understands the appeal of rock gathering. Around you have a series of rocks. Rocks in the camp, rocks on the road. In BLM land, scattered camps are often lined with rocks that people collect during the winter. Snowbirds, which inhabit Arizona and other warm-climate regions, make rock jewelry and cut and polish rock. They collect fossils and search for gems. Some snowbirds search for gold and go to the desert with their gold-washing equipment. Others look for turquoise in desert soils or ancient turquoise mines.

Rock hunters have every opportunity, and when camping or exploring fun trails, it's almost impossible not to give in to the urge to collect them.

Outdoor Tasks and Rock Collection

But you don't have to go camping to start collecting rocks. Anyone wandering outdoors may want to pick up rocks along the way. Visit a park, forest, or beach, and you might pick up a bright orange rock or a nice quartz or agate. Before you know it, your pockets are full of stones, bags, and buckets. It's definitely easy to get addicted to extraction.

Serious and Occasional Rockhounding Collectors

If at any time you are interested in rocks, you know that there are serious rockhounds and also that they collect casually.

Serious rock hunters learn to identify rocks and minerals and carry their field guide, rock beak, and staff on their belts. They know how to differentiate between agate and quartz. The collections are carefully classified by name and type and are marked with the date and place of discovery. Serious hounds often attend rock and mineral shows, trade-in taxidermy, and have their own cutting and polishing equipment. They should not be taken lightly.

Casual collectors are completely different from rock collectors. They rarely know the names of the rocks they have and classify their collections with names like "shiny black rocks" and "pretty pink rocks." They collect by walking in the desert or on the beach, and they collect everything that catches their attention.

However, both types of rock collectors love these stones, fill their RVs and houses with rocks, accumulate rocks in every available space, and always want a nicer rock.

5 Reasons to Collect Rocks

Picking up rocks is very good for both children and adults. There are many reasons why it's a great hobby:

- **Collecting rocks is cheap!** Rocks are free if you pick up yours while walking!

- **Rocks are available!** You can find rocks on the beach, in the mountains, by the lake, in the desert, or the driveway!
- **The rocks are fun and beautiful.** Each rock has a different color, shape, texture, and consistency; some are beautiful.
- **Rocks have a history.** Some rocks contain fossils that tell the story of prehistory and the earth's formation.
- **Stones are useful.** Rocks have been used as tools and building materials since the beginning of civilization, but collectors can also turn them into jewelry and ornaments.

Some Uses of Rocks

Some may consider this a silly and useless pastime, but rock collectors as they know that these, which we collect everywhere, have many good uses. Here are some of the many uses of rocks:

The first knew what could become useful objects spears, arrows, hammers, mortars, jewelry, and beads.

If there are rocks such as granite, marble, and travertine (a type of limestone found in thermal areas), the slabs are cut and used for building materials, floors, and corridors.

Obsidian is a black volcanic glass used to make scalpels, knives, beautiful wind chimes, and carvings.

Granite and marble are used in sculptures, tombstones, buildings, and monuments.

Jewelry is made with many different rocks and minerals.

The home has items such as photo frames, clocks, paperweights, bookends, figurines, and ashtrays, which can be made of petrified wood, jade, turquoise, and other rocks and minerals in beautiful colors and designs.

Large boulders end in benches, sculptures, lawn ornaments, and landscaping focal points.

Creative Uses for the Small Rock Collector

When you like to accumulate rocks like me, you may need some excuse to pick up another rock. So, I made a list of more creative uses for these collected stones.

- Use rocks to decorate some flower beds.
- Put rocks in decorative baskets or dishes at home.
- They can be a beautiful paperweight.
- Keep some rocks on hand to defend yourself.

- Nice rocks to put in fountains or indoor planters.
- Hide a key under a rock.
- Place some in your aquarium.
- Place some of the plants in the pots of indoor flowers.
- Fill a cute vase with colored rocks and place water to bring out the colors.
- Cover the edges of massifs.
- Stick some cork or felt inside and use it for door stops.

Rock Grabbing Inspired by Lucille Ball

Lucille Ball and Desi Arnaz long ago starred in a movie called The Long, Long Trailer. A story full of hilarity and adventure while they go around the country in a trailer. Lucy becomes fascinated by rocks and starts picking them up and putting them in the caravan. Although Desi warned her, she followed, and, in the end, they were rolling all over the camper.

As you can see, collecting rocks is a passion, and if you are here, surely you have that vein to look for yours, but you want to know how it is done.

CHAPTER #2
HISTORY OF ROCKHOUNDING

Rock hunting was already very popular before the media and the Internet era. In the 1930s, Native Americans and other amateur geologists traveled to the mountains and deserts to collect, carve, and polish stones such as agate, jasper, and petrified wood.

The Great Depression played its part in the popularity of rock hunting. Unemployment drives people to explore quarries, canyons, and fields to dig up gems or anything of value that can sell for an extra dollar. These rock hunters then set up roadside rock shops where they sold their finds to tourists or vacationers.

Today, people get involved in rock hunting for a variety of reasons. Some see it as an entertaining way to learn more about the history and geology of a given area. Jewelers do this to find unique items to add to their creations.

Others (such as hikers) are dedicated to enjoying the immersive experience and becoming familiar with nature. It is a hobby enjoyed by many people of all ages.

For example, the annual rock search in Canada is conducted in Bancroft, Ontario. Every August, thousands of hounds, geologists, and hobbyists flock to Bancroft (Canada's mining capital) for the Rockhound Gemboree.

There Are Many Stories

In the days shortly after the Civil War, soldiers marched west in hopes of making a fortune. The legends of Lewis and Clark, John Colter, and the trapper who traded in the famous Pierre Hole are well known, and there are good historical indications that explain the area's importance. But the story of the individual miners and pioneers who came to search for gold is shrouded in more mystery. These secrets can still be found in the Northern Rocky Mountains if you know where and what to look for.

The geologically rich states of Idaho, Wyoming, and Montana are like pirates' treasure chests; Gold, sapphire, opal, amethyst, jade, quartz, garnet, and topaz are just a few of the many gems of the region. After all, Idaho is known as the "Gem State" for a reason:

72 types of gemstones can be found there. Montana is known as the "Treasure State" because of its rich mineral deposits, including two desirable varieties of blue sapphire: Yogo and Fancy Montana Sapphire. The complex geology of the Greater Yellowstone area includes everything from dinosaur bones to petrified forests; Yellowstone National Park contains samples covering 540 million years, from Cambrian to Cenozoic.

Searching for rocks involves finding and collecting specimens of minerals and fossils. Not only is this a fun and often rewarding way to spend the day, but it's also a great way to learn more about the area and the minerals that call it home. For those interested in trying, here are some starting points.

The chain of lakes is the perfect base camp for those interested in the wild experience and is the only place in the United States where the continental divide has split, creating a circular basin where water does not flow into the Pacific or Atlantic. From there, Crooks Gap is a 30-mile loop of pure Wyoming wilderness filled with sagebrush, pine trees, ponds, and salt flats that make up the formation of the chain of lakes. The area is famous for wild Red Desert horses, and hikers can appreciate the diverse population of migratory birds. Of course, you can find a lot of jade along the walk. These green specimens exist as pebbles and boulders on alluvial fans and the ground. The appearance of emerald is softer than that of ordinary rock and looks as if it has passed through a rock container.

An Amateur's Story

The day Alison Jean Cole learned to cut rocks at a club in her area changed her life. "It's the best thing I've ever done in my life," she said in an interview. "I spent the night and then came back every day for a few months." Soon after, she quit and began working as a full-time quarry. Six years later, Cole is a professional gem hunter, rock prospector, and miner who has rock and mineral specimens that she collects in extensive fieldwork and guided jewelry tours. Hunting in the Pacific Northwest.

Rockhounding, the recreational search for interesting rocks and minerals in geological formations, originated in the mining heritage of the American West and became a national pastime in the late 1950s and early 1960s, although, as I said before, it goes back a long time after the Civil War. With the opening of related clubs throughout the country. Today, a new wave of young rock-hunting enthusiasts is embracing the hobby of reconnecting with nature and unplugging their phones. The trade attracts all kinds of newcomers, from homemakers and jewelry designers to businesswomen and engaged city girls.

"My club has doubled in size in recent years," she said. "When I first joined, they were mainly old white retirees with very conservative worldviews. Now, there are many young and free people, which is a very interesting change." on social media with an explosion of Facebook pages, a dedicated Instagram hashtag, and even a Rockhounding meme.

According to Cole, rock hunting is "the easiest sport in the world," but what does it take to master this fascinating craft truly? You will know later with my professional advice for you to choose correctly.

Scientific Research and Rockhounding Help Uncover Fascinating Treasures and Stories

Learn what attracts and keeps people's interest in rock hunting, mining history, and mineralogical research as varied as the natural discoveries they make.

For Canada's Jason White, it could be said to go back to his days as a Boy Scout in St. John's, Newfoundland. During this time, a Scout leader gave him a book about Newfoundland's mines written in the 1950s. Perhaps in the late 1990s, he made his first claims when he knew nothing of his work but was passionate and enthusiastic about his business. It can be found. It could also be when I was looking for full-time prospects and selling vegetable and herb grafts to pay for fuel to travel to the excavation site. Or these moments and many others led him to where he is today, continuing to explore one of his most important discoveries, amethyst from the La Manche mine.

The Mining Legacy

The La Manche mine consists of four mines located on the west side of the Avalon Peninsula adjacent to the former community of La Manche in Newfoundland, Canada. Technical writer White researched the mining and cultural history of the area to develop a program of activities for the mine. He explained that the La Manche mine was officially discovered in the 1850s, but long before that, locals collected lead in the area for weight fishing. Evidence of mining attempts in Placentia Bay dates back to the sixteenth century (the Basques, French, Spanish, Portuguese and British were the first Europeans to explore the area).

The first mining attempts in the 1850s were the work of a company owned by transatlantic communication cable developers and employed Cornish miners. The vein extends two miles inland from the seafloor at Placentia Bay and is 4 inches wide at 16 feet, with the deepest axis sinking to 400 feet. According to White's research, historically, the first official mining attempts were made by the same people responsible for the transatlantic cable in 1855 and 1864.

La Manche's connection to amethyst, while the focus of White's current mining and research activities, can be traced back to the Newfoundland Geological Survey of 1868, which discovered amethyst at the La Mancha mine. Unlike many things, the 1920s were not favorable for mines, as the main shaft extended 400 feet, but in 1929 the dam broke and flooded the mine, and with the market crash the following month, it was impossible to improve repairs to the damage.

History of Maine Tourmaline

1820 would be one of the key years in Maine's history. That year, Maine was granted statehood, becoming the 23rd state in the United States of America. That same year, tourmaline was discovered in the mountains of western Maine.

Augustus Choate Hamlin, son of one of the original discoverers, Elijah Hamlin, spent much of his life exploring the Mica Mountains in search of a hidden treasure. He also carefully documented his father's work, as well as himself and others, and his 1895 book History of Mica Mountain gives us a full account of the original find, so vividly that it was The Link Behind Time until the fall of 1820. Their work is considered our primary source of information on tourmaline discoveries in Maine.

The discovery was made by two students interested in mineralogy who spent most of their free time searching for minerals on the exposed cornices and mountains around Paris, Maine.

On a clear, quiet day in the late autumn of 1820, Elijah Hamlin and Ezekiel Holmes began to walk the chain of hills that formed the eastern boundary of Paris and extended to the northwest.

They spent most of the day on Mica Mountain, in the mountains south of the city, and headed home down the west slope, fifty miles or more after the sun went down. On the horizon further west. Young Hamlin hesitated for a moment at the top of the mountain to admire the mesmerizing view before him, and as he turned east to take one last look at the forests and mountains behind him, a green flash flashed on an object. A tree whose roots were knocked down by the wind caught his attention.

Walking there, he found a transparent green crystal scattered on the ground, stuck to the fallen tree's roots. The student excitedly grabbed the gleaming gem and shouted to his classmate that he had already climbed to the top of the hill and was not far below the slope. After reviewing what they had found, the students searched the surrounding soil for other specimens, but the rapidly growing twilight forced the young mineralogist to abandon the search. However, they decided to return early the next morning and continue their exploration, but overnight a storm hit and covered the hill and adjacent fields with thick snow that continued into spring.

As soon as the winter snow melted, the hills and slopes were exposed, and the students began their search again, this time successfully. They went straight to the raw edge of the mountaintop outcrop, which they had not examined until nightfall. As they climbed the rock, they were astonished to see many crystals and crystal fragments scattered on the exposed rock face, shining in the sunlight. These they put together carefully; they tracked the others to the ground beneath the ledge, formed by the rock breaking and eagerly rummaged through the ground for hidden treasures. More than thirty crystalline and beautiful crystals rewarded the students' work, who, with joy and amazement held them in the sunlight and admired them in various shades of green, red, white, and yellow. They stumbled upon one of nature's most abundant and rare laboratories.

News of the find reached the villagers, many of whom rushed to the site and obtained some fine specimens as trophies or souvenirs, but the exact nature of the find remains unknown, even to the original discoverers. Some specimens were sent to Yale professor Benjamin Silliman, and only then were they first identified as tourmalines. In 1826, Hamlin published a description of the early gems, revealing his skills as a competent amateur mineralogist. In 1822, Hamlin's younger brothers, Cyrus and Hannibal (later Abraham Lincoln's vice president), who were teenagers, borrowed some blasting tools and performed abrupt blasting and blasting on solid ledges. His efforts paid off, discovering some of his time's largest and best quality specimens. They collected more than two dozen crystals of various green and red colors, some more than two inches long and more than an inch in diameter.

News of the tourmaline discovery spread quickly, and Mica Mountain quickly became the most important mining area in North America, with rich and diverse mineral wealth.

Tourmaline has been mined in Maine for nearly 200 years, but today Mount Mica is still considered to have the greatest potential for different crystal and gem production. An important discovery was made there in 1978 when a great gem-quality crystal was discovered in a grapefruit-sized cavity: one of the cut gems was an impeccable 256-carat blue-green, 4–5 times larger than the previous "largest gems in the area."

In 1972 a World-Class Discovery Was Made

Plumbago Mountain was discovered in 1972 and is now recognized as the largest gem discovery in North America. The now-famous discovery was made in August 1972 by George Hartman, Dale Sweat, and James Young, and after mining and initial exploration, Hartman, Sweatt, and Dean McCrillis formed Plumbago Mining Corporation. They obtained a lease from International Paper, hired Frank Perham, and resumed exploration of gem tourmaline, opening in October 1972 a series of pockets that were richer than those discovered. In Maine, and maybe anywhere in the world.

Mining operations at Plumbago Mountain continued until 1974, and details of early discoveries are available through vivid descriptions in Dean McCrillis' journals.

2003 to Present

Mt. Mica, the site of the first tourmaline discovery in Maine in 1820, continues to produce beautiful green tourmalines, and a private collector has been mining there since 2003. In 2006, the mine produced unusually large pink tourmaline crystals.

There are indications that Mica Mountain may reproduce two decades of gem crystals. Maine is a gem-producing state; as Frank Pelham, Maine's mining "dean," said, "it has a lot of life left in the old state."

2009—Eureka Blue

In 2009, Plumbago Mountain made headlines again with its blue tourmaline ring that caught the attention of gem collectors worldwide. Blue has always been the rarest color among tourmalines, and this discovery is the only blue that has been well-received by the gemstone world.

Starting in September 2009, a series of pockets were opened in the Graphite Mountains, which threw up a treasure trove of blue-green tourmaline, the color of the twilight sky.

A unique cutting style was developed to highlight these gemstones' best color and brilliance, known as "Eureka" tourmalines. The "twilight" cut takes advantage of tourmaline's unique properties of producing color, seamlessly combining the color and brightness of the gem into facets of cascading rows and columns that awaken color and light with the slightest movement.

The "mascot" of Eureka's discovery was "Owl," a mineral specimen with an unusual tourmaline crystal structure and a host mineral resembling the face of an owl. The owl has two large blue tourmaline eyes and two bright feathered white Clevelandite crystals. The head is brown owl lepidolite.

On February 15, 2010, Presidents Day, a large bag of gems was opened, which included an incredible 120-carat blue tourmaline crystal. Known as the "President," it was eventually cut and polished into nine gemstones ranging from 0.50 carats to 24.76 carats. This great gem was a gift from Maine to U.S. President Barack Obama when he visited the state. One miner was horrified by the idea that tourmaline was thought to help bring peace, and if it helped bring peace to the world so that The President of the United States could possess the gem, which would be correct to do so. This gem is the largest ever found in Eureka.

Maine has long been known for its unique watermelon tourmalines. This rare combination of two tourmalines in a single crystal has also been found elsewhere, such as in Brazil, but the best specimens were found in Oxford County, Maine.

First discovered at Dunton Quarry in Newry in 1902, watermelon tourmaline crystals consist of a large core of dark red tourmaline surrounded by a layer of green. Famed Maine naturalist George Howe named the gem 70 years later; crystals have been discovered like never before in exciting work at Plumbago Mountain, which for the first time, has produced crystals with gem-quality color and transparency.

Gem-quality watermelon tourmaline has been used for many artistic purposes. Glass "logs" can be sliced like a loaf of bread and then polished well on each side. Watermelon tourmaline "pieces" have been the focal point of many pieces of fine jewelry, and artwork has been carved from this material.

The bicolor tourmaline from Maine is even more unique: the crystal turns green at one end and pink at the other. Mineralogists could not determine what natural force caused the dramatic color change during crystallization. Some rare gems have been found to have a bicolor characteristic of blue to green, and some tricolor gems with different shades of gray, green, and blue.

The findings, wealth, and rock search come from ancient times. However, they were not sought, although they were known that there were different rocks underground, it would be until the nineteenth century that it would begin to be given series, and during the twentieth that, amateurs appeared, and both professional and amateur geology gained strength.

CHAPTER #3
LAWS AND REGULATIONS

Collecting rocks, although it is a hobby or a profession, is not outside the law; it must comply with a series of rules that seek to preserve the spaces where it is explored. In this chapter, I will discuss them depending on the different sites.

The legality of collecting rocks, minerals, and fossils in public spaces depends on which of the four federal agencies has authority in the area. Collecting rocks, minerals, and fossils are not allowed in most scenarios. However, certain types of public land allow it to be searched with certain restrictions.

Finding out what kind of public land you find on and which government agency is in charge, it's the first step in determining whether collecting rocks is allowed. I will delve into each type of public land and the specific laws and regulations that describe whether rock hunting is allowed and, if so, what restrictions exist.

Rockhounding on Public Lands

When collecting rocks, minerals, and fossils, the landowner must obtain permission to collect a sample, no matter how small or large. The default assumption should always be that you should not collect specimens in the field unless given permission. It applies to private land and millions of acres of public land in the United States.

In the United States, four major federal agencies manage approximately 640 million acres of land owned by the U.S. government:

- **Bureau of Land Management (BLM):** has 245 million acres (12% of U.S. land).
- **National Park Service (NPS):** 85 million acres (3.5% of U.S. land).
- U.S. Fish and Wildlife Service (USFWS): 95 million acres (4% of U.S. land).
- **U.S. Forest Service (USFS):** 193 million acres (8% of U.S. land).

It should be added that there are 14 million acres of state parks and many local parks. Together, they account for more than 28 percent of all U.S. land.

That's a lot of space for you to look for rocks! These millions of acres are divided into 15 main types: 13 types of federal lands and state and local parks.

Typically, recreational rock hunting for your collection is more likely to be done on lands operated by BLM and USFS than on NPS and USFWS. It is because the types of land they manage are often intended for use by the general public, and in spaces like national parks, there are designated spaces for it to protect from damage.

I'm going to talk about the legal status of rock, mineral, and fossil collections for every type of public land because, no matter where you are, you know what the regulations say.

Generally, national parks prohibit the collection of rocks, minerals, fossils, or other specimens. The only exception is the limited manual collection allowed in some Alaska park units. Another exception is approved scientific research that requires prior authorization.

It's easy to get frustrated because the National Park System doesn't allow the collection of rocks and other specimens, but keep your mission in mind. Their mission is to protect some of our country's most unique and special parts, and geology makes them special. If everyone brings home fragments of parks, their natural beauty will quickly degrade.

Regulation

"The collection, washing, and washing of gold, whether for recreational or educational purposes, are generally prohibited by all units of the National Park System. Those who break these rules are subject to criminal penalties."

National parks don't just prohibit the collection of specimens. Many tangent-related activities are illegal (external link), including using metal detectors, throwing stones down hillsides, and digging specimens.

Exceptions and Details

Other than scientific research licenses, the only exception to the national park rock search rule is "in some Alaskan parks (not Klondike Gold Rush, Sitka, Denali, Glacier Bay, and Katmai), using non-disruptive methods (e.g., no peaks), managers may stop collection if it has a significant adverse impact on park resources and visitor enjoyment."

National Forests

National forests are one of your best options for collecting rocks. USFS generally allows unlicensed people to collect rocks, minerals, and fossils. USFS operates 154 national forests and 20 grasslands, leaving ample land for rock hunters.

However, there are some limitations. USFS has some exceptions regarding the types of materials it can collect (including historical artifacts and meteorites) and the scope and methods of its operations. There are also places where harvesting is not allowed, such as private mining concessions.

Notable and established mining sites already exist in many of these national forests, but you are not limited to these. You can search for your own specimens almost anywhere on the USFS! Gold washing is allowed and is an activity that is very popular in many USFS locations.

Regulation

"On land in most national forest systems, a limited collection of rocks and minerals for personal use is allowed. These materials may be collected without permission as long as the collection is for personal, hobby, and non-commercial use."

Exceptions and Details

Collecting rocks, minerals, and fossils in USFS spaces is legal but not without restrictions. These exceptions usually relate to where, what, how, and how much you collect your materials.

- **Mineral claims:** There are certain privately owned mineral claims on USFS land that you cannot collect without the express permission of the claim owner. The local USFS office will list these claims and their location.
- **Wilderness areas:** The USFS designates special areas too sensitive to this type of activity.
- **What you collect:** You cannot collect any items with historical or archaeological relevance, meteorites, or petrified wood.
- **Material quantity:** The USFS allows a reasonable amount of material to be collected, loosely defined as approximately 10 pounds or less.

National Wildlife Refuges

Collecting minerals, rocks, or fossils is almost universally forbidden in the National Wildlife Refuge. These are areas designed to protect fish, wildlife, and their habitats while allowing people to enjoy them. Understandably, the USFWS has made it illegal to collect geological specimens from these areas, as this could negatively affect wildlife there.

Regulation

"The unauthorized destruction, disfigurement, injury, disturbance or removal of any public space, including natural objects or private property, from any national wildlife refuge is prohibited."

"Unless otherwise provided by law, prospecting, locating or displaying mining conces-sions within the National Wildlife Refuge is prohibited."

Exceptions and Details

After some research to find exceptions to the "do not collect" rule, I found one.

Kofa National Wildlife Refuge has a designated area of 1.5 square miles called Crystal Hill; it is famous for the quartz crystals it possesses. Only those sought as recreation are allowed, excavation is not possible, and only 10 specimens or 10 pounds can be captured in 12 months.

National Areas of Conservation

The National Reserve is managed by the Bureau of Land Management and is therefore open to recreational rock hunting. There are 16 of these types (plus 5 very similar types) in these regions, most of which are in the western U.S.

There are some specific areas where sample collection is prohibited. Of course, the com-mon BLM usage limitations regarding collection methods, volumes, and specific types of findings apply to all of them.

Regulation

"Hand tools, including pans and metal detectors, can be used to search for gold and sil-ver... Recreational searches that do not involve mechanical equipment are permitted in wilderness areas and wilderness study areas, provided they do not cause disturbance to the surface or harm the environment."

"Gemstones and common rock specimens can be collected from unclaimed sites for private use."

"Reasonable amounts of fossils of common invertebrates, such as plants, mollusks, and trilobites, can be collected for personal use, but not marketed or sold."

"Up to 25 pounds of petrified wood plus one piece per person per day, and up to 250 pounds per person per year. Items over 250 pounds require a permit."

Exceptions and Details

While much of the National Reserve's land is open to rock, mineral, and fossil collection there are some important exceptions and limitations to keep in mind:

- Red Rock Canyon and Sloan Reserve are not allowed to be searched.

- Don't take anything from private mining concessions.
- Restricted area and mining lease records can be viewed at the BLM office.
- You can get a "reasonable amount" of BLM land material.
- You may not sell or trade the materials you collect.
- Excavation or alteration of the surface is not allowed.
- Vertebrate fossils cannot be collected.
- Cultural materials such as arrows and artifacts cannot be removed.

National Monuments

National monuments differ slightly from previous areas because they are not administered by a single government agency. Depending on your location, any of these four agencies can manage them (NPS, USFS, USFWS, and BLM) and several others.

While you might think this would make rock collection regulations more obscure or complicated, the answer here is simple. You are not allowed to collect rocks, minerals, or fossils in national monuments, with 1 very specific exception. It makes sense, given the nature of national monuments, which commemorate and protect areas of great historical value.

Regulation

The exact rules depend on the services that govern the national monument and, in many cases, the specific monument itself, and I won't list them all here. However, as some examples:

- **BLM:** "Not allowed in BLM-administered National Monuments."
- **USFWS:** "Collection, including antlers, rocks, bones, artifacts, and plant life, is prohibited."

Exceptions and Details

- **NPS:** Pipestone National Monument gives Native Americans permission to collect catlinite (red stone).
- **USFS:** I found no exceptions that permit searching for rocks in a USFS-run National Monument.
- **USFWS:** I found no exceptions that permit to search for rocks in a USFWS-administered National Monument.
- **BLM:** I found no exceptions that permit to search for rocks in a BLM-run National Monument.

National Historic Sites

National Historic Sites are virtually managed by NPS, except for Grey Towers National Historic Site, which USFS operates. These areas are designed to preserve or reflect the appearance of a place during its most important historical period.

The size and scope of National Historic Sites depend on what they protect: some sites are tasked with protecting more than one important historical event or person. Due to the historical importance of these sites, logging of any kind is not allowed, without exception.

Regulation

Unless otherwise provided in this chapter, the following acts are prohibited:

Possess, destroy, damage, disfigure, remove, excavate or disturb its natural state:

- Fossil and non-fossil paleontological specimens, cultural or archaeological resources, or parts thereof.
- Mineral resources or cave formations or parts thereof.

Provisions "prohibit the possession, destruction, disturbance of mineral resources in park unit."

Exceptions and Details

I found no exception to these regulations. Collecting rocks, minerals, and fossils at any National Historic Site is illegal.

National Recreation Areas

Rock collection laws can be confusing for National Recreation Areas because these areas can be managed by any of the 3 federal agencies: NPS, BLM, and USFS. Whether you collect rocks, minerals, and fossils will depend on the agency managing your location, and in some cases, the rules will vary from place to place, even within the same institution.

If you are on NPS land, you are out of luck: tracking rocks is not allowed, with one exception (see below).

If you are on BLM land, you can collect samples if the area is underdeveloped. If you have any questions, please check with your local BLM office.

For USFS-managed national recreational areas, the same rules apply to national forests. You can collect rocks, minerals, and fossils with certain restrictions.

Regulation

- **NPS:** "All units of the National Park System generally prohibit the collection, gold mining, and gold laundering of rock, mineral, and paleontological specimens for recreational or educational purposes. Violators of this prohibition are subject to criminal sanctions."
- **BLM:** "Rocks, semi-precious stones, and minerals may be collected for free or licensed on public land managed by BLM, provided that... unless authorized by BLM, the collection is not done at a developed recreational site or area." Designated as a rock search area.
- **USFS:** "On land in most national forest systems, a limited collection of rocks and minerals for personal use is allowed. These materials may be collected without permission as long as the collection is for personal, hobby, and non-commercial use."

Exceptions and Details

- **NPS:** Recreational gold washing is permitted in Whiskeytown's recreational spaces.
- **BLM:** The rules state that certain recreational areas developed or off-limits to rockhounding cannot be used. You probably can if you're on undeveloped land away from people, but I recommend checking with your local BLM office.
- **USFS:** I found no special exceptions for national recreational spaces, so they seem to fall under the same general rock-finding rules as national forests. The usual limitations on how much you can charge, the method of collection, and restrictions on mining concessions still apply.

National Battlefields

When you say "national battlefield" the truth is that it includes four subcategories of federal lands: national battlefields, national battlefield parks, national military parks, and national battlefield sites. It may sound pedantic, but I just wanted to clarify this for anyone reading this and wondering if they are the same.

All fields where there were national battles belong to the National Park Service and therefore have all the usual NPS land restrictions. The collection of rocks, minerals, and fossils is prohibited on the National Battlefield. Given the nature of these sites, I certainly don't think it's unreasonable: we should treat these areas with the respect they deserve and leave everything as it is.

Regulation

'Unless otherwise specified... The following acts are prohibited:

Possesses, destroys, injures, disfigures, subtracts, excavates, or disturbs its natural state:

- Fossil and non-fossil paleontological specimens, cultural or archaeological resources, or parts thereof.
- Mineral resources or large formations or parts thereof."

Regulation "Prohibition of possession, destruction, disturbance of mineral resources in the park units."

Exceptions and Details

I found no exception to these regulations. Collecting rocks, minerals, and fossils any-where on the national battlefield is illegal.

National Deserts

In the national wilderness, you find one of the most protected spaces in the United States. It can be administered by any of the four major federal land management agen-cies, but in all cases, the pursuit of rocks is prohibited in the state's wilderness areas.

National Wilderness Areas are often larger public lands, so it's important to know exactly where you are and where your biggest conservation measures begin. For example, most BLM land is open for rock hunting, but if you veer into the wrong area, the law may not allow you to gather there.

Regulation

- **NPS:** "Unless otherwise noted... The following is prohibited: Possession, destruction injury, disfigurement, removal, excavation, or alteration of its natural state:
  - » Fossil and non-fossil paleontological specimens, cultural or archaeological re-sources, or parts thereof.
  - » Mineral resources or large formations or parts thereof."
- **USFS:** "It is not allowed to collect rocks in Wilderness Areas."
- **USFWS:** Regulations do not allow minerals of common variety to be extracted... ir wilderness areas, recommended wilderness areas, and proposed wilderness areas.
- **BLM:** "The exceptions say that specifically... wilderness areas."

Exceptions and Details

I found no exception to these regulations in the country's wilderness areas.

National Wild and Scenic Rivers

National Wild and Scenic Rivers is a special space of public lands used to protect the natural state of rivers and surrounding lands. They can be administered by any of the four major federal land management agencies.

Typically, rock hunting is permitted on national natural and scenic rivers managed by BLM and USFS but not on rivers managed by NPS and USFWS. It is in line with the general policies of these respective agencies.

Regulation

The Bureau of Land Management or the U.S. Forest Service may allow non-commercial minerals to be taken out for entertainment (e.g., hobby collection, rock hunting, washing, or dredging), depending on the number, size, and scale of the collection. Activities are subject to affect resource values and river management objectives. This series is subject to state, local, and other federal regulations. Commercial and non-commercial local minerals are generally prohibited by the National Park Service and the U.S. Fish and Wildlife Service (FWS) Fishing (under valid existing rights). For sanctuaries in Alaska, FWS, according to 50 CFR 36.31(b), allows manual washing of gold on the surface for recreational use only.

Exceptions and Details

The usual BLM and USFS limitations on quantities, methods of taking out, and private mineral claims still apply here. Alaska's USFWS-managed rivers allow for artisanal recreational gold mining. I can't find an exception for NPS to manage rivers.

National Coasts and Lakeshores

The United States has 10 national coastlines. Except for one on the Atlantic coast (except Point Reyes, California). There are also three National Shores, all on the Great Lakes. NPS manages all 13 sites, so searching for rocks to manage them is simple and rigorous. Rock, mineral, or fossil collection is prohibited at National Seashore and Lake Shores.

Regulation

"The collection, gold mining, and gold washing of rock, mineral, and paleontological samples for education or entertainment are generally prohibited by all units of the National Park System. Those who break the rules can face legal sanctions."

Exceptions and Details

I found no exception to the NPS's National Lakeshores and Shores rock hunting. The collection is not allowed.

National Trails

National trails are a relatively large group of diverse types of protected trails that can be managed by various federal and state, or local agencies. They typically overlap and are linked to other protected areas, such as national parks, so rock-chasing laws are complex and vary from place to place, even on the same trail.

Regulation

The national trails' regulations are too complex to cover here because they vary from place to place, even on the same trail. However, you can be assured that any trail owned or even partially managed by NPS will follow the same rules as national parks, so rock theft will not be allowed.

NPS: "Several components of the service-administered national trail system have been designated units of the national park system. Accordingly, these trails are administered as national park areas and are subject to all policies contained herein and those contained in the National Trail System Act. Subject to any other specified requirements. Another scenic, historical, connecting/transverse, and recreational trail designated under the National Trail System Act is located on or near the park unit. The service may also manage some of these, though not as national park system units. The service will work with other land managers, nonprofits, and user groups to promote."

Exceptions and Details

The only way to know if there is a rock track in a particular spot along the National Trail is to identify who manages the land and ask them directly. These trails are often co-managed by multiple entities, complicating current regulations.

State Parks

Parks are managed by individual states, which means there are 50 different sets of laws and regulations for collecting rocks, minerals, and fossils. It makes it difficult to know what is allowed in a given state park regarding harassment rocks.

State parks cannot collect rocks, minerals, and fossils, but there are some caveats.

City Parks

There are thousands of urban parks in the United States, each regulated by its respective city. Rock hunting rules vary by location, but as a general rule, you should not damage or move public property. Unfortunately, this will include rocks. Check with your city to see if they allow this activity in any or all parks.

CHAPTER #4

BEFORE YOU BEGIN: EVERYTHING YOU NEED TO KNOW

The information I present in this chapter will allow you to enjoy the tour, find a wide variety of spaces to travel and get the most out of each destination.

The Importance of Bringing Information About Interesting Places to Go Rockhounding

Mindat (Mindat.org): The Initial Research Tool

It is a site that will surely interest you; when you enter, you will see in the search bar options to find, for example, the map that opens for you and that you can enlarge, so you choose a certain site, then you can see some minerals from that area as well as other relevant information.

A detail that cannot be overlooked is that if you see a camera icon next to some minerals and press it, you will see images of it.

But what is Mindat?

It is a free public mineralogy database created by Jolyon Ralph in 2000. It claims to be the largest database and mineralogical information site on the Internet. In addition to having information about minerals, it also has information about biology.

The beginning of Mindat was with a database that Jolyon Raph used for himself in 1993. In 2000 it registered the domain name www.mindat.org and made a public call for cooperation on October 10 of that year. Months later, the database had grown to sizeable and included thousands of photographs. While pseudonyms can be used, the vast majority of contributors use their own names to prevent vandalism. As of July 2010, 220,000 sites have been reached, and 320,000 photos have been taken. It is currently part of the Hudson Institute of Mineralogy.

At the heart of the Mindat, the structure is a database of 5,453 minerals (as of September 4, 2018) recognized by the International Mineralogical Association (IMA), whose official name is in English. Each new mineral released is added immediately. As a complement, there are 42,842 mineral names, including translations in different languages, varieties, outdated names, etc. Mineral searches, which can be conducted in any language, provide a page with key attributes and access to a list of regions by country, and within each country follows a geographic hierarchy with details by country.

USGS, Is a Very Powerful Tool, the Most Underused Tool!

It is another tool that contains a lot of information and where you can do a cross-check with Mindat because although the previous one has a great wealth of content, it is good to cross it with the conditions of those spaces to know what you will do once you go to that destination by rocks.

Keep in mind that the USGS (United States Geological Survey) is a scientific office that is part of the United States Department of the Interior. It has scientific information about natural hazards that can put lives, livelihoods, energy, water, minerals, and other natural resources and the environment at risk. Scientists are developing methods and tools to provide relevant, timely, and useful information about land and processes.

Special Advice

When looking at the maps, don't forget to check the elevations you'll find on the way to your site. Changes of a few hundred feet or more can be a strong round of cardio! You can see the elevations of the spaces. Even just by using the satellite map, you can find interesting places. For example, in Washington, some ridges on the predominant side of the wind may be bare, and the satellite will show mineralization on the surface.

You Can Find a Lot of Information Also in Museums and Universities

The universities and museums dedicated to rocks contain a piece of very broad information about it; I recommend that before making a set of hammers and picks, you document yourself and visit these sites, either in the city or on its pages, Canada has a wealth of museums to visit online if you are not physically present and in the United States, there are also many options.

One of the great joys of this hobby is that it offers lifelong learning opportunities. There's more to learning about rocks and minerals than the joy of finding, seeing, touching, and doing things with rocks and minerals. There are many resources out there. It is just a small example to start with.

To this end, museums acquire, preserve and exhibit mineralogical and geological samples, artifacts, and documents relating to the history and mineralogy of the area in question. The museum also acquires and exhibits archaeological and paleontological specimens and other objects of interest.

The Franklin Mineral Museum, for example, is a nonprofit educational institution located at Evans Street, Franklin, Sussex County, New Jersey. Created for educational and scientific purposes only, the museum was established on June 2, 1964, and opened its doors to visitors on October 9, 1965. Like this, there are many others, and each one has a wide variety of rocks, according to the area it exhibits, as they stand out in a theme or mineral to combine with history. Surely in your city, you can visit several museums for a weekend or as a family. You're sure to learn new things.

Lean on Geology Course

Geology courses would help once you understand where the rocks come from, how they were formed, etc. It will help you know now where to look and find. If you are interested, you can learn and discover all the world that hides behind those rocks.

Geology studies the earth, its processes, materials, history, and its impact on people and life. Stones, crystals, mountains, earthquakes, volcanoes, rivers, glaciers, landslides, floods, and many other topics fall into this broad field of study.

Geologists work to understand the history of our planet. The better one can learn about Earth's history, and the better one can anticipate events and processes from the past that may affect the future. Although surely your plan is not to become a geologist, it is good that you know at a general level about the subject. Here are a few examples:

- **Geologists study Earth's processes:** landslides, earthquakes, floods, and volcanic eruptions, among many other processes, can be dangerous to humans.
- **In addition, they study materials from the earth:** People use materials from the earth every day. They use oil produced in wells, metals produced in mines, and water extracted from streams or underground.
- **Geologists study the history of the Earth:** Today, we focus on climate change. Many geologists are working to understand Earth's current climates and how they have changed over time.

If you're curious about the planet we live on, especially finding those cool rocks, you have the potential for a discipline that combines the best of art and science, and geology is a good course to learn more about.

Studying geology will give you many tools not only for the area but also for understanding life. Geology, for example, is a very intuitive science. Many problems in geology are a lot like solving puzzles. A common task for students is to develop possible explanations for the events that produced the surrounding landscape.

If you've ever wondered how a certain hill came to be in a certain place or why a large rock outcrop is exposed in a particular way, a geology course can help you understand these features and discover them. Once you understand geology, you will see the world around you in a new light.

The Importance of Joining Rockhounding Clubs

If you are passionate about going to a field, sitting down, starting to dig and clean various rocks to see if you find that beauty you are hunting, let me tell you that you are not alone because many like you share this passion and surely address the same doubts, fears, happiness, passion and desire to find something inside the earth.

All over the world, there are many clubs, and it is just a matter of looking for them and encouraging you to join one; it would not seem strange to me that in your city and closer than you imagine, there is one where you join and be part of a fraternity that is hunting the same as you.

What can I find in such a club if I only go looking for rocks to have at home?

I will answer you with an example; I paraphrase the information that the CFMS has, which is the Federation of Mineralogical Societies of California.

The Federation aims to disseminate mineralogy and earth sciences knowledge and promote research in these disciplines. To achieve this, we:

- It represents merged and unincorporated mineralogical societies and their members to promote a better understanding of geology, mineralogy, and rocks.
- It provides rock and mineral samples from various California, Nevada, and Hawaii locations.
- The society may request educational video programming to complement its monthly educational programming.
- Provide the community with a list of educational speakers on gemological and mineralogical topics for programming via Zoom or other presentation platforms.
- Provide field trips for all societies to participate in exploring, researching, and collecting specimens.
- It provides a monthly newsletter to the societies that give information on the ongoing activities and services of the member societies.
- Maintain a scholarship program that provides financial assistance to eligible students majoring in Earth Sciences or Gem Arts and Jewelry.
- Teaching courses in gem arts and jewelry.
- Encourage young people's interest in geology and mineralogy.
- Organize an annual gem and mineral exhibit to familiarize the public with rocks gems, and minerals.
- Support public museums to host mineral and gem art exhibitions.
- It provides member societies of the California Federation of Mineralogical Societies with a liability insurance plan for their members, which includes tours, shows, lectures, and more.

As you can see, you have some benefits when joining a club.

The Importance of Climate

If you have plans to go out this weekend to look for rocks, you have to look at the weather forecasts, as it might not be the one you expect and take a bad time. Imagine that you go out to look for rocks and you find a storm or a cyclone alert in the area, which will make you sit for a long time, contemplating the window and with the weak faith that it rages and you can go out to look for rocks, not to mention what may happen to look in the mud or that is not your thing and seems more difficult. If you're starting, consider all of this. Winter is not the best time to look for rocks, but I will leave you some tips in the next section.

Winter Is Not the Best Season, but There Are Some Tips

- Winter could sometimes become the best place to rockhound if you look at beaches after winter storms (because the wind and waves of a good storm will always stir up new rocks to find). The waves bring some fossils from the bottom, or the sand is removed and altered, which means you will fish in a troubled river, only on a troubled beach. Keep this in mind if you are going to go for rocks and you are near a beach.
- Another great tip for you to go for rocks in the winter is in the beds of the streams, especially just after a good thaw; the reason is that this process is called frost wedging and is one of the biggest drivers of erosion, which opens possibilities for you to dig and find.
- Explore areas that are generally too hot (for example, the southwestern part of the US), where you can have great potential to find rocks.
- Take advantage of the winter to do everything you can't do in the other seasons (because you're busy looking for rocks). Routine paperwork, declarations, and economic projects allow you to live later in the season when you look for rocks. Winter is the ideal time to organize, label, and catalog the collection, even if you have found rocks in summer and other seasons.
- If you want to create a business with your rocks, you can use the winter to sort and organize the rocks, select those you sell, and then find a buyer.
- If you collect raw jasper or agate, you can look to cut them out of time. It just depends on the equipment you have access to. Trimming saws are small and affordable but somewhat difficult, like all gem machines. For stones only a few inches wide or smaller, they are a perfect way to enter the wonderful interior of a rock. Real panel saws are very expensive, but you can usually make money selling other rocks from the collection. People crave unique and beautiful gems; others are valuable when you go through the process. It's also fun to open any geode you've collected. You'll be the first to look inside; they're easy to cut.
- Cabochons are domed and semi-precious stones. Much of it is used in jewelry, but large pieces of high-quality material are a beautiful display. Cutting a cabochon is an art, but many people learn the basics quickly. The idea is to caress a piece of material, shape it with an abrasive grinding wheel, and sand the dome until a nice belt remains. Then comes the enamel. Cabachon machines are expensive but can machine

smaller materials with a Dremel and the right drill. You can also sign up for rock clubs, many of which have special member spaces.

- If you like sparkles, then you will love falling rocks. The turner passes the stones through straight grains until they are rounded and highly polished. Many specimens look great this way, and glasses are more accessible to the average person. The main problem is usually noise rather than space or clutter. Revolving stones can often show striking patterns, but the main goal is to remove the substrate and make it shine, not "artificially" change the shape of the stone by cutting and carving.

- Winding is one of the easiest ways to make your gem wearable. Many rockers also do some goldsmithing, but it's a full-fledged hobby in its own right and not as available. Wire wraps can range from simple to complex fine jewelry, but most of the wraps you'll see can be made without specialized equipment. A few pliers, a few wire cutters, and a few turns of wire can do amazing things in the hands of the right artisan.

Do not miss the winter; take advantage of it by planning your next trips to do in spring and study the places on mindat.org, which, as I told you before, have a piece of very comprehensive information; I do not doubt that it will be your first-hand tool to go out every day to look for rocks.

CHAPTER #5
BEFORE YOU BEGIN: WHAT YOU MUST HAVE

I know you like to walk comfortably, with ample clothes and soft shoes, but looking for rocks requires that you wear special clothes so that the experience is not painful or, in the event of an incident, you are protected. I explain in this chapter how you should protect yourself when looking for stones and additional tips according to various related elements.

Clothes

To begin with, the clothes have to be special, not simply that you put on those jeans that you have in the closet and that is a thick fabric, although the intention is fine, it is not the best protection you can have, there are better alternatives, and you must consider variables such as the weather, where you go, the difficulty you will find to reach that site and the mobility you will have.

I leave you a tip you will surely thank me for in the field of work: choose pants with built-in knee pads. It will be an immense relief, I assure you.

There's a reason jeans became the standard uniform for California miners. They are resistant, very hard, easy to wash and dust, and perfect for rock lovers. Whatever the temperature, jeans are the way to go. You'll find yourself sitting in a hole, on a mound, or the side of an outcrop. Wear jeans to stay comfortable and avoid scratches or injuries. But like I said, put one with knee pads.

Shirts

Suppose they are long sleeves better, for protection against mosquitoes and other insects and sun protection. A long-sleeved t-shirt with a short-sleeved t-shirt on top is stylish and very protective.

The t-shirts, long-sleeved shirts, jeans, etc., that I suggest for rock hunting can get dirty quickly. With each adventure, the life of the wardrobe is shortened. Therefore, I suggest you buy quality clothes to withstand the days. Garments of almost any size abound, especially shirts and jeans. If in the future you have to throw away a t-shirt or jeans and buy second-hand, it is better for your expenses and more responsible with the environment; it is already a second-hand item.

Glasses

Glasses, glasses, glasses for everyone! When you hammer rocks, fragments fly. Protective glasses, blue light blockers, or sunglasses are an absolute requirement. Just like in a workshop class, don't start breaking rocks without using this protection.

Safety glasses are a good choice for wholesale purchases. If you're going on a group adventure, there's a good chance someone won't. These are necessary for the safety and accountability of the entire rock hunter community. Always bring yours and remind your people to bring theirs.

Hat

Hat, chapeau, or cap. No matter what you call this item, your rock hunter uniform is an invaluable resource to help protect you from the sun and keep your hair healthy in this activity that requires all your hand-eye coordination.

Gloves

Gloves are a must, whether industrial or fabric and available at any hardware store or convenience store, or gas station. Your hands will thank you and your manicurist too.

Cost-effective gloves are cloth and cloth gloves commonly found in neighborhood stores or auto supplies at any pharmacy or convenience store. They are inexpensive, and you may want more than a pair to share with other rock hounds.

Earplugs

It is a personal preference and depends on your sensitivity to noise. Rocking rocks or using jackhammers (extreme stone chases) all day can be exhausting for your hearing. Some Rockhounds are immune to loud noises and don't need them, but others require earplugs for comfort and prevention. Maybe bring headphones, as they're small enough to take up almost no space in a backpack.

Skin Protector

Protect yourself from the sun every day, bloodhound! You can stay in the shade all day or sunbathe. Protect your skin beforehand with SPF (a good tip every day), and keep some travel sunscreen on hand for other hounds who may not have yours.

Notebook and Pen

Notebook and pen to help you document your discoveries and where they come from. Another chapter details the importance of documenting your findings and the added value of documenting them emotionally and financially. Your phone is a great tool, but a small notebook and pen or pencil may be easier.

The Orange Vest That Stands Out

When hunting rocks on outcrops next to county or state roads where rock hunting is allowed, consider a fluorescent orange or yellow mesh vest for safety. For example, Pennsylvania is a state that allows the pursuit of rocks, but no chasing of rocks is allowed on American or federal highways, or highways drivers are interested in what you are doing (this is common). Some public areas where rock hunting is allowed are areas where hunting is allowed. For example, we look for geodes, private property, acres outside private farms in southern Indiana, and back to state forests in Indiana where seasonal hunting is allowed. We also have rock hunting in Texas and Georgia on private land where hunting is allowed. In short, this vest will allow you to be located easier in case it is necessary.

Safety Boots

I will stop for a moment to talk about very important boots because you will use them a lot transporting you from one side to the other and putting yourself in situations where they are a fundamental grip.

You have to know that hiking boots are the basic element when looking for rocks and have to be quality. Therefore, I will show you their parts:

- Cushioning.
- Quick loop rings, stainless.
- Rigid helmet for finger protection.
- High resistance cord.
- Padded cane collar.
- The average density for damping.
- Double and triple sewn.
- Flexible anatomical midsole with longitudinal twisting for greater control.
- Exterior is in a waterproof leather.
- Hook with a self-locking system.
- Waterproof/breathable membrane.
- Sidewall. Supports the foot in the singing.
- Removable, absorbent, and breathable insole.
- Added protection for midsole seams.
- Rigid support to wrap and protect the heel.
- Soles with non-slip engraving.
- Handle to put on shoes.
- Padded area to increase comfort.

Rubber is the most commonly used element. Depending on the sculpted material and the design, we will have more or less grip on wet or icy ground. These soles are sculpted to expel mud and elements that can adhere. The distribution of the different densities of the sole, mainly of the heel, will help us to cushion the impact of the foot against the ground. In some models, this effect is achieved with an air chamber under the heel. The soft cushioning sole transmits a perceptible wave from the sole to the lower part of the quadriceps (thigh), while in all technical soles, they barely reach the knee.

The sculpted design of these soles allows the heel to hold the boot and not slip on the descents, while on the climbs, better traction is achieved thanks to the shape and resistance of the toe and sides to provide a better grip of the foot. Avoid sprains and injuries caused by uneven terrain.

Some soles have suitable toe and heel flanges to attach crampons with self-fixing.

Like car tires, the rubber used to make shoe soles ages with time, cold, heat, oxidation, and ultraviolet light. The result will be a hardening of the material, which will cause a loss of adhesion.

Some boots have a membrane sock between the inner lining and the outer shell, combined with the heat sealing of the seams and the protection of the area of the metal hooks, making the boot completely waterproof while allowing the necessary perspiration of the foot.

It should be noted that this membrane will gradually fail when combined with boots of different materials and acid in the sweat of the feet. Repeatedly bending when walking, being overweight, and slipping on the foot can also have the same effect, which can cause micro-tears inside the material. That is why the membrane will lose its total reliability after 3 or 4 years, depending on the treatment. They are materials that meet strict international quality standards, but we cannot ask impossible.

The minimal thickness of the thermal material, commonly found in alpine boots, insulates the feet from the cold outside without adding extra bulk or weight and provides a better feel on the ground.

In the case of plastic boots, the inner lining is separated from the outer layer and is removable. In addition, plastic boots are specially designed for alpine and extreme conditions due to their thermal insulation ability.

Several types of fur can be used to make hiking boots.

For the manufacture of leather mountain boots, healthy animal skins should be used and only selected from the best areas, such as the back, to meet the high demands demanded by the optimal performance and durability of our materials.

Choosing the Best Boot

This is according to usage:

- If you are doing a small climb in the mountain and just want to get closer to nature, walking on trails, you should choose hiking boots or hiking.
- If you want your shoes to serve for gentle weekend walks and be able to get anywhere comfortable and safe, your boots will be hiking boots.
- If you are looking for a shoe that reaches higher and can step on snow or ice without problem, you can put crampons on them, which protect you better from the cold; in this case, your boots will be a mountain.
- However, if your project is more ambitious and you want to conquer peaks in extremely cold conditions, you should choose boots classified as High Extreme Mountain.

With all this, I want to tell you not to wear your shoes at home or normal boots to go to the mountains. They are elementary and key to a good experience.

Tools

Some tools cannot be missing on your trip to look for rocks; I will tell you why you should have them and the qualities of each one.

Uncommon Tools

These are some tools you need and will not find in any list.

- **Egg cartons**: These will be in a dry and well-protected place so that you can place small rocks inside each space that fit and are protected.
- **Newspaper**: The newspaper will allow you to have other rocks protected; if you get several and wrap them, you can have them under protection so that you can carry them without worries.

Tools That Every Rock Finder Should Have

- **A flashlight (night hunting):** There are many models of flashlights for night hunting; you have to have a quality one that illuminates well and helps you enter dark spaces and check the rocks; they also have to be durable or rechargeable so that they do not leave you stranded.
- **A magnet:** Meteorites and ferrous rocks (such as magnets) attract small handheld magnets, such as refrigerator magnets. (A metal detector could be a good investment for someone serious about collecting Ethereum, gold, or other metals.)
- **UV light (short-wave and long-wave) and display bag**: Used to identify fluorescent minerals. You can use a black plastic sheet instead of the observation bag.

- **Camera**: With the cameras, you can document everything you do, take pictures of some rocks, and have that file that you then have in your space at home.
- **Phone with GPS**: It is a good choice for a compass and altimeter. So you can always locate yourself and be clear about where to go.
- **Pen and notebook**: I recommend keeping track of where you found each piece and the details you want to put.
- **Books**: It never hurts to document or consult any doubt, so have books (like this one) with you so you can review and have the voice of the experience at hand.
- **Water bottle**: As well as other foods, you must stay hydrated and well-fed; choose healthy food that keeps you satiated and takes up little space.
- **Spray bottle**: Water jet bottle for you to wash a rock or confirm if it is worth it; when you are in full work, you may find a piece and not know if it is really good or not, then you wet it a little and clean it, and so you confirm.
- **A bag of resistant rock**: I take this opportunity to leave you a valuable tip. If you have hunted or have access to a bird hunting bag, take it with you, it is the best option to collect and transport large rocks. There you can put all those treasures you fish, although, if you find someone to carry those rocks for you, my respects, carry that friend, that is why you took him.
- **Magnifying glass**: Choose one of those magnifying glasses of small jewelers, but with great magnification, it will help you to see the traces or lines in the rocks and identify those more reluctant to give their names.
- **Small wire brush**: Sometimes, there will be rocks full of stuck lumps that do not come out when you shake them, so the wire brush, soft and soothing, will allow you to remove most of it, although careful not to scratch the rock.
- **Rock hammer:** Hammers are necessary, and on the market, there is a variety of them; you need even one to move small bushes and large rocks since it is not surprising to get scorpions and other dangerous animals underneath.
- **Cracking hammer**: Another of the hammers is the one that will help you make the smaller large rocks; you can make one chisel that is perfect for rockhounds. A hammer and a separate set of chisels work best when precision is most important, such as when you chisel around a crystal to remove it from the rock that is a host.
- **Brushes:** Brushes, on the other hand, are a key part of every rock hunting kit. Its main requirement is durability; besides, most brushes are good enough to remove dirt from rocks. It will serve to discover behind the mud what is hidden.
- **Plastic organizer box**: Some things will help you collect rocks and minerals. Every Rockhound handles its findings differently, but a plastic organizer is always an option if you don't already have a way. It facilitates the organization of minerals, but its real value was not immediately obvious. I know many hounds, and they enjoy different parts of the process: research, hunting, analysis, and polishing. However, one thing that rock hounds aren't always particularly good at is showing.
- **Bucket**: You will need it when you have a lot of lands around and want to put it aside and have more workspace or put things inside.
- **Screwdriver or Flintstone**: Some rocks are reluctant to get out; this tool will allow you to bite, pry, and release this piece for your collection.
- **Waders**: Choose those totally waterproof and made of good material so that if you

get caught in the rain, they keep you dry and warm. A wide variety of models on the market; will help you increase protection while hunting rocks.
- **Rake:** Have a rake in your set of tools, which will serve you in areas such as river beds or lakes; sometimes, you have to move a pile of stones to get the ideal.

All the tools are important; I recommend you take them with you, but the best thing is that if you like to talk, you can go with a friend, it is the best company, and together you can enjoy the landscape and have fun.

Security Tools

Many security tools cannot be missed:

GLOVE AND BACK GLOVES

Safety gloves are perfect for you to start your exit, although before I recommended them, now I tell you that you must have some backrest, in case you lose one and choose resistant, there are those with hard knuckles to weave better or very resistant models and at the same time ergonomic to allow better mobility.

FIRST AID KIT

Always carry a first aid kit in your backpack as a basic material when you search for stones in the mountains. It has little weight, takes up space, and can help you with small but uncomfortable surprises.

First aid training is also strongly recommended, as such training can save lives in the event of an accident.

Here's what you should put in the medicine cabinet:

- Analgesics for general pain and lower fever: Paracetamol. Also, a more powerful analgesic for treating more intense pain (appendicitis, dental, fractures, etc.) or an injury with a hammer or a rock.
- Antacid for stomach pain.
- Eye drops for cleaning and soothing eye diseases (sun, snow, etc.).
- Diarrhea: loperamide.
- Nausea and vomiting: metoclopramide.
- For mild allergic reactions: Dexchlorpheniramine.
- Cough: Codeine.

To clean wounds:

- Sterile needles.
- Two elastic compression bandages of 5 cm.
- Surgical tape.
- Sterile gauze.

- Povidone iodine antiseptic solution.
- Scissors.
- Approach strips.
- Sticking plasters.
- A 10 ml tube of saline.
- A greased gauze to put on a wound before covering it.
- A small clamp.
- A few scalpel blades.

To prevent other problems:

- Some energy food (extreme tiredness).
- Sun cream total protection.
- Sterile gloves.
- Glucose pills (exhaustion).
- Tablets to purify water.
- Mineral salts (dehydration).
- A thermal blanket (for you to shelter the wounded).

Always carry a leaflet of all medications or a summary of their indications and dosages in your medicine cabinet. Also, remember to update them periodically and check the expiration dates.

Tick Repellent

A tick repellent is a liquid applied to skin, clothing or other surfaces to prevent ticks from crawling on those surfaces.

Ticks can spread disease-causing bacteria. Using a tick repellent can reduce the likelihood of being bitten by a tick, reducing the risk of spreading these diseases.

Snake Alligators

If you are in rattlesnake territory, you must have this element to identify them and move them away in case you see them. Beware that it is the most poisonous in the world.

CHAPTER #6
WHAT IS A ROCK?

Surely while reading this book, you have begun to ask: What is a rock? Maybe you think that the answer is very simple, but "rock" is a common word and a scientific term, and this sometimes causes confusion about whether certain things should be called rocks or not.

In geology, a rock is defined as:

- A solid mass.
- Natural.
- Made of minerals or mineraloid matter.

In this chapter, I will talk about what a rock is so that you clearly understand what you will look for in the forest.

Geologists believe that rocks are made up of one or more bonded minerals. Generally, rocks are composed of several minerals, although some are composed of a single mineral.

Rocks found in the earth's crust are distinguished from each other by their origin. There are igneous, metamorphic, and sedimentary rocks; I will tell you extensively about them shortly. Igneous rocks are formed by the cooling and solidification of magma, a mixture of molten rock and gases found at high temperatures in the Earth's interior. Metamorphic rocks can be formed from the transformation of sedimentary or igneous rocks.

Metamorphism is the process of changing the mineralogy and structure of existing rocks through the action of heat and pressure. Metamorphic rocks can also be formed from another type of metamorphic rock. Finally, sedimentary rocks are formed by pre-existing decomposing rocks and then deposited as sediments (unconsolidated) through transport such as water, wind, and glaciers. When these materials are buried deeply, they fuse and form sedimentary rocks.

What Types of Rock Are There?

There are three types of rocks: igneous, metamorphic, and sedimentary.

Igneous

Igneous rock is the result of the cooling and solidification of magma. A process that can occur within the crust, producing plutonic or intrusive igneous rocks, such as granite, gabbro, etc.; or, when in contact with the atmosphere or ocean, it can produce volcanic or extrusive igneous rocks, such as basalt, rhyolite, or obsidian.

Igneous rocks (from the Latin word for fire) are created when hot molten material cools and solidifies. Igneous rock can also be made in several different ways. They are called intrusive or plutonic igneous rocks when formed deep within the earth. They are called extrusive or volcanic igneous rocks in case they form outside or on the earth's crust.

Granite and diorite are clear examples of common intrusive rocks. They have the texture of coarse mineral grains, suggesting that they cooled within the Earth over thousands or millions of years, a time course that allows for the growth of large mineral crystals.

Alternatively, rocks like basalt and obsidian boast minimal grains and a somewhat fine texture. It happens because when magma turns to lava, it cools faster than if left inside the Earth, allowing crystals to form in less time. Obsidian cools rapidly and turns into the volcanic glass as it is ejected, making the particles invisible to the naked eye.

Extruded igneous rocks can also have a blister-like or "porous" texture. It happens when the ejected magma still has gas inside, so the bubbles are trapped when it cools, giving the rock a bubbling texture. An example of this is pumice.

Granite contains long minerals in the form of plates initially dislocated, but when enough pressure is applied, they rotate to point in the same direction they were compressed into a flat plate. When granite goes through this process, as at the boundaries of tectonic plates, it turns into gneiss (pronounced "pleasant").

Rocks that are not hardwoods form in the same way, but they do not have minerals that tend to line up under pressure, so they do not have the appearance of layers of leafy rocks. Sedimentary rocks such as bituminous coal, limestone, and sandstone, with sufficient heat and pressure, can become phyllode metamorphic rocks such as anthracite marble, and quartzite. Non-foliate rocks can also form through metamorphism, which occurs when magma comes into contact with surrounding rocks.

Metamorphic Rocks

Metamorphic rocks are created when igneous or sedimentary rocks are subjected to prolonged heat, moisture, and/or pressure exposure. It is how granite becomes gneiss, limestone becomes marble, and schist becomes slate. Metamorphic rocks are unusua in geologically young regions such as Costa Rica, while rocks are common and abundant in the Cordillera, such as the Andes.

Metamorphic rocks have changed their original shape due to tremendous heat or pressure. There are two types of metamorphic rocks: foliate and non-foliate. When rocks with flat or slender minerals are subjected to great pressure, the minerals are arranged in layers, forming foliations. Foliage is the arrangement of elongated or layered minerals (such as amphiboles or mica) perpendicular to the direction of the applied pressure. An example of this transformation can be seen in granite.

Sedimentary rocks are formed due to atmospheric factors acting on existing rocks. Weathering caused by the physical, chemical, and biological agents to which the rock is subject weakens and breaks it, and the products or sediments produced by the rock are transported by wind and rivers to other places, where they are gradually stratified. The rocks produced by this process are sedimentary rocks, which can be clastic, such as sandstone, shale, and conglomerate, or chemical or evaporitic, such as limestone and halite.

Sedimentary

Sedimentary rocks are generated from fragments of other existing rocks or organic matter. Sedimentary rocks are divided into clastic, organic (biological), and chemical. Clastic sedimentary rocks, such as sandstone, are formed from clasts or fragments of another rock. Organ sedimentary rocks, such as coal, are formed by the compression of hard biological materials, such as plants, shells, and bones, into rocks; the formation of clastic and organic rocks begins with the weathering or disintegrating of exposed rock into small fragments. These fragments are removed from their source through erosion processes and transported to new locations by wind, water, ice, or biological activity. Once the sediment settles somewhere and accumulates enough, the lower layers come together to form solid rock. Chemical sedimentary rocks, such as limestone, rock salt, and flint, are formed by chemical precipitation. A chemical precipitate is a compound, such as calcium carbonate, salts, and silica, that forms when the solution (usual water) in which it dissolves evaporates, leaving the compound behind. It happens when water travels through the earth's crust, eroding the rock and dissolving some of the minerals it contains, transporting them elsewhere. When water evaporates, these dissolved minerals precipitate.

The Lithological Cycle

You know three types of rocks: igneous, sedimentary, and metamorphic. You also learned that all of these can change. Any rock can change and become another class. These processes usually occur slowly. Some of the changes take place just below the Earth's surface. Some changes are ostensibly universal. These are part of the rock cycle. The cycles, how they formed, and how they changed. I speak to you in this subchapter precisely of that whole cycle.

Process of the Lithological Cycle

There are three main types of processes that change a rock:

- **Cooling and crystallization**: Deep in the earth, the temperature is so high that they produce magma. As the magma cools, the crystals grow and form igneous rocks; the crystals get bigger if the magma cools slowly or stays deep in the Earth. If the magma cools quickly, the crystals are very small. The formation of crystals from magma is called crystallization.
- **Wear and erosion**: Water, wind, ice, and even plants and animals can wear down rocks. Over time, they can break up larger rocks and turn them into sediments. Rocks break down in weathering; thus, flowing water, wind, and glaciers carry these fragments from one place to another. It is called erosion. Eventually, the sediment is left or deposited somewhere. This process is called sedimentation, and the tank can then be compacted and cemented. It forms sedimentary rocks. This whole process can take hundreds or thousands of years.
- **Metamorphism**: The word means "shapeshifting." It changes shape if the rock is exposed to extreme temperatures or pressures within the crust. Due to metamorphism, the rock does not melt completely. Rocks change due to heat and pressure. Metamorphic rocks may have new compositions or mineral textures.

The cycle has no beginning and no end; it is constant. The processes involved in the lithological cycle take hundreds, thousands, or even millions of years. While rocks are solid and immutable to us, they change slowly over time.

What Determines the Value of a Gemstone?

Gems or gemstones are minerals, rocks, or materials processed to make jewelry. Its use dates back to ancient times when jewelry began to be used as a symbol of worship, power, exclusivity, or decoration. Do you know what features can increase or decrease their value in the market?

Different properties must be considered to determine the value of gemstones, such as their hardness, guaranteeing their durability, thus increasing their value in the market.

Speaking of the hardness of a mineral, it is inevitable to mention Friedrich Mohs, who in 1825 established a scale with 10 reference minerals, to which he attributed a certain hardness. The scale begins with talc, which has a hardness value of 1, and ends with diamond, considered one of the stones with a hardness value of 10. Mohs designed the scale to show that one mineral can scratch another, less hard mineral, but vice versa.

In addition to the mineral's hardness, another factor that can increase or decrease a stone's value is its color. Throughout history, many colored gemstones have been thought to have healing properties, which is why they are especially popular with collectors.

Emeralds, Rubies, or Sapphires Are Considered the Most Popular Gemstones, Along With Diamonds

Vibrant, bright, uniform colors can increase a stone's value compared to other colors with various shades. Some stones have characteristic colors, such as ruby, due to some of their components, such as iron and chromium. This colored gem takes its name from the Latin "rubber," which means red. Another gemstone with high market value and characteristic green color is emerald because it contains chromium and vanadium.

Color aside, we focus on another important characteristic when analyzing gemstones: weight. At this point, it is necessary to distinguish the difference between size and weight. Just because one gem is bigger doesn't necessarily mean it's more valuable, as it can also be lighter than the other.

One Carat Is Equivalent to Approximately 0.2 Grams

The weight and purity of gemstones are measured in carats (one carat equals 0.2 grams), a Greek word referring to the carob tree, whose seeds were used in ancient times to determine the weight and value of gemstones.

Color, brightness, transparency, scarcity, tonality, hardness, size, weight, symmetry, and composition. In valuing any gemstone or gem, all the piece's characteristics are thoroughly analyzed, and, finally, they will be analyzed as far as possible. Establish its true value in the marketing process.

CHAPTER #7
LET'S LEARN ALL THE DIFFERENT TYPES

I have been talking to you since the beginning of rocks to put on such boots, clothes, pants with knee pads, picks, hammers, chisels, flashlights, and everything you need to enjoy this hobby, but we have not talked about rocks, especially those that interest us, from gems to fossils, so in this chapter, I will explain a little about each one.

Precious Gems

Some gemstones have a high value; surely you have heard of them:

Diamond

Diamond is a pure carbon mineral crystallized in the cubic crystal system. You may have heard that it is the hardest mineral known in nature. It has a score of 10 out of 10 on the Mohs scale. Another diamond can only scratch a diamond. At the same time, it is interesting to talk about the fragility of diamonds. It cannot be scratched, but it can break, and if it is struck where it is peeled, the diamond will crack, leaving a clean, flat scale. Very curious! It would be unfortunate, but it is good to know that diamonds are not indestructible.

The most popular diamonds are colorless, free of impurities, and well-cut. The highest quality diamonds are those used in jewelry. Abandoned, used in certain industrial sectors, they are not gem quality.

Emeralds

Emeralds belong to the beryl family. The most precious emerald has very few inclusions (called "garden" in the jewelry) and must have an intense green color due to the presence of chromium in its composition. Colombian emeralds are well known and appreciated, although other origins, such as Brazil and Zambia, also have quality gems.

The degree of hardness on the Mohs scale is 7.5–8 out of 10.

Ruby

Ruby belongs to the corundum family. The most appreciated are those of bright red color and without inclusions. It is a precious gem, you may have heard of pigeon blood rubies, but they are very scarce and may be overrated.

Ruby is a very hard mineral, almost at the level of diamonds. It has a Mohs hardness of 9 out of 10. Fine rubies above a certain size are even more expensive than diamonds.

Sapphires

They also belong to the corundum family, and the most popular sapphires are those that have a deep blue color. Nature has provided us with other colors of sapphire, which are also beautiful, but blue sapphire is the most valuable.

On the Mohs scale, it is as hard as a ruby, 9 out of 10. The mines with the best sapphires are in Kashmir, not to mention Ceylon sapphires. In ivory, we have sapphire rings that will leave you speechless.

Minerals

There is a very wide series of minerals; I have divided it by colors, then I leave you a couple of examples of each one with its qualities.

Black Stones

Black semi-precious stones are very beautiful pieces because their color makes them look like they are from another planet. The predominantly black gemstones are emerald, garnet, onyx, agate, black jade, or rutile quartz.

Onyx

Onyx is a dark agate that varies in color from black to red with alternating white streaks. It is composed of silica and is of volcanic origin. The word onyx comes from the Greek word "onux," which means "nail" or "claw," of its color. Onyx forms in silica deposits at low temperatures as silica-rich water seeps through cracks in other rocks.

Deposits: India, the United States, Mexico, Brazil, Russia, and South Africa.

Jet

Jet is a lignite with a high carbon content. Due to its organic origin, it is considered a mineraloid. Jets are typically formed in rocks of marine origin from wet wood buried in the ground and subjected to high pressure. It is light, black, or brown and sometimes contains small shiny pyrite inclusions. Previously used as a talisman, the powder spray was believed to have medicinal properties and was taken with water or alcohol.

Deposits: Spain (Asturias, Teruel), India, Russia, England (Whitby), Germany, Poland, Turkey, France, the United States, Portugal, Mexico, and Venezuela.

Red Stones

In addition to rubies, some semiprecious stones have the color red in their main index and are considered gems. Zircon, coral, garnet, feldspar, carnelian, fire opal, or spinel, to name a few, stand out.

Zircon

Zircon is a type of zirconium silicate. Its most common color is reddish brown, but it can also be yellow, green, or colorless. It usually contains traces of other elements such as uranium, lead, thorium, and hafnium. It is considered to be the oldest mineral in the world.

The name Zircon is derived from the Arabic "zarqun" and the Persian "zargun," meaning "golden," about one of the colors it can take. It occurs as small crystals in igneous, metamorphic, and sedimentary rocks.

In geology, zircon is used for the radiometric dating of rocks containing it. It is also often used to make sand for foundry and industrial abrasives.

Deposits: Sri Lanka, Brazil, Australia, Cambodia, South Africa, Thailand, Myanmar, the United States, Russia, and Madagascar.

GARNET

Garnets are a group of 15 different types of minerals. Although they vary in color and chemical formula, all garnets have a cubic crystal system, usually forming dodecahedrons, trapezoids, or a combination of both.

Among the most abundant garnets are garnet (red or pink), pyrope (red or orange) spessartine (yellow, orange, or red), and garnet (green, red, orange, brown, yellow, or white). When cut into cabochons, garnets sometimes have a star-shaped optical effect It is due to its possible inclusion of rutile. The name garnet comes from the Latin "granatum" (endowed with the grain), which refers to the red fruit of the pomegranate.

Deposits: Thailand, Brazil, the United States, Madagascar, India, Sri Lanka, Canada, and Russia.

Pink Stones

Pink is a rare color in nature. As a result, this dominant color gemstone is scarce and also very precious. Examples of pink gemstones are topaz, kunzite, Malay garnet, morganite or rose quartz.

TOPAZ

Topaz is an aluminosilicate formed by the release of fluorine during the crystallization of igneous rocks. It is commonly found in pegmatites, rhyolite caves, and hydrothermal veins. It forms well-developed crystals and is often used as a gem in jewelry.

Topaz comes from the Sanskrit word "tapaz," which means "fire." Its name is also related to the ancient topaz island in the Red Sea, now the island of Zabargad (St. John's Island, Egypt), where the first specimens are said to have been found.

Topaz comes in different colors and varieties, pink topaz, yellow topaz, blue topaz, brown topaz, and colorless. The imperial topaz or golden topaz of Brazil is a particularly appreciated variety.

Deposits: Brazil, China, Zambia, the United States, Afghanistan, Russia, Sri Lanka, Madagascar, and Namibia.

Morganite

Morganite is a gem-quality pink beryl. This color is due to the presence of manganese or cesium. Yellow or orange morganite can also be found, which often shows colored bands.

Morganite usually forms plate-shaped crystals and exists in pegmatites.

Morganite is named after the American banker and collector JPMorgan Chase.

Deposits: Brazil, Russia, Italy, Madagascar, the United States, Mozambique, Pakistan, and Afghanistan.

Yellow Stones

Yellow gemstones may not be that precious in jewelry, but they are great visually. Gemstones of predominant yellow tones include citrine, lemon quartz, tourmaline, spodumene, and sphene.

CITRINE QUARTZ

Citrine quartz is a variant of yellow crystalline quartz. The coloration is due to the presence of hydrated iron oxide. It forms hexagonal crystals and is commonly found in pegmatites and hydrothermal veins. Its name is derived from the Latin "citrinus," which refers to its color. As a rarer type of quartz than other types, heat-treated amethyst and smoky quartz are sometimes used to obtain natural-looking citrine quartz.

Deposits: Russia, the United States, India, Great Britain, Madagascar, Brazil, France, and Germany.

TOURMALINES

Tourmaline is a group of mixed crystals in the borosilicate family, consisting of 11 species including plover (black), elbaite (pink, red, green, blue), and dravite (brown). The elbaite is the most valuable species due to its colorful varieties, and the most famous is indigo (blue), rubellite (pink or red), watermelon tourmaline (pink interior and green surface), and Verdelite (green).

Tourmaline is characterized by their composition differences, even though they have the same crystal structure. The black and opaque tourmalines known as plover and cathedral are the most abundant. Its crystals are usually colorful and are commonly found in pegmatites, granites, hydrothermal veins, and gas stone veins. Tourmaline is a mineral used in industry that has piezoelectric properties.

Deposits: Brazil, Russia, Afghanistan, India, Namibia, the United States, Canada, Mexico, Africa, and Madagascar.

Green Stones

In addition to the well-known (and analyzed) emeralds, there are other semiprecious stones in which bright greens predominate. The most precious green gems are alexandrite, amazonite, malachite, hectorite, enstatite, aventurine, chrysoberyl, apatite, amphora, turquoise, peridot, emerald or larimar, name a few.

AMAZONITE

Amazonite is a blue-green micro clinic crystal system and is one of the most abundant feldspars. Its crystals are prismatic and are usually arranged in multiple twins, but they can also appear in large numbers. Amazonite is characterized by its scaly texture, called exolysis. It is said to take its name from the Amazon River, although there are no clear indications of the presence of Amazonians in the Amazon region.

Deposits: Brazil, Great Britain, Russia, the United States, Ethiopia, Kenya, Madagascar, Namibia, India, Zimbabwe, Spain, and Austria.

MALACHITE

Malachite is a secondary copper mineral that occurs in grape-shaped or embedded blocks, usually in a fibrous structure, although it can also occur in kidney-shaped aggregates with concentric bands and stalactites; more rarely, it occurs in individual prismatic crystals.

The main characteristic of malachite is the various shades of green that can be seen when cutting or polishing it, making it a mineral often cut into cabochons for jewelry making.

Malachite is considered one of the most important minerals in human history due to its direct involvement in the development of metallurgy, professional skills, and organized labor, and it was later discovered to be converted into primary copper after being melted in fire (4000 BC).

In ancient Egypt, Malachite was used as eye makeup, a pigment for jars and glass, and as an amulet. We also find ancient sources that tell us about the medicinal properties of malachite, for example, in work "Psyca" by Saint Hildegard of Bingen (twelfth century).

Deposits: Zimbabwe, Colombia, the United States, Hungary, Namibia, Morocco, Zambia, Russia, Romania, Congo, South Africa, China, Australia, and France.

Blue Stones

Blue is usually a strange color in nature. But in addition to sapphire, other stones have this color, which is a true geological wonder. We have lolita, topaz, moonstone, lapis lazuli, eagle's eye, chrysoprase, aquamarine and fluorite, and many more that we see in green gems but that can also take a gem of blue tone.

RAINBOW MOONSTONE

The rainbow moonstone belongs to the group of feldspars and is considered a milky white orthoclase. Its name refers to its resemblance to the moon, so it refers to its brightness.

It exhibits a light iridescent color with blue and gold tones, called white light. This brightness is due to the crisscrossing of the albite and orthoclase scales it contains.

Deposits: India, Myanmar, Sri Lanka, Brazil, Australia, Tanzania, and the United States.

LAPIS LAZULI

Lapis lazuli is a deep blue mineral because it contains lapis lazuli. It is associated with white inclusions of calcite and pyrite, which give it its mottled golden appearance. Lapis lazuli is a stone that has long been valued for jewelry making with a long and ancient tradition. Lapis lazuli has been found in the tombs of Egyptian pharaohs. It is also used in monuments, jewelry, ornaments, utensils, and as a pigment for works of art from different eras and cultures.

The name lapis lazuli comes from the Latin "lapis," "stone," from the Persian "lazhuward," "blue," and the Arabic "lazaward," "sky." It usually occurs in compact blocks, rarely in the form of implanted rhombic dodecahedrons.

Deposits: Chile, Argentina, the United States, Afghanistan, Russia, Italy, and Egypt.

Violet Stones

Semi-precious violet gemstones are also very valuable. Examples of purple gems are, for example, amethyst, spodumene, chalcedony, tanzanite, sodalite, or lepidolite, as well as other gems that we have already seen that can take this color.

CHALCEDONY

Blue Chalcedony is a type of microcrystalline quartz; it can be papillary in the form of grapes or stalactite. It occurs in hydrothermal veins and volcanic and sedimentary rocks. Blue chalcedony is white when pure but a different color when it contains inclusions of other minerals. When chalcedony has clear bands, it is called agate.

Deposits: Brazil, Romania, Namibia, Japan, Portugal, Turkey, the United States, and Malawi.

Tanzanite

Tanzanite is a deep blue-purple zoisite. It takes its name from where it was discovered in 1976 in the Merari Mountains in northern Tanzania.

Tanzanite is characterized by its pleochroism, which allows seeing the mineral in different colors depending on the observation position and lighting. From dark blue to light blue, gray, and purple, colors can be seen.

White Stones

The absence of color can also attract attention. It's not just diamonds that prove it, but these semi-precious stones. White gemstones, such as garnet and certain varieties of quartz and moonstone, are generally highly prized in the world of jewelry and art.

Howlite

Howlite is a calcium borosilicate hydroxide. It usually forms numerous white nodules threaded by veins of other minerals, and although rare, the crystals are plate-shaped.

Howlite was named in 1868 by Canadian chemist Henry How.

Deposits: The United States, Mexico, Germany, Canada, Russia, and Turkey.

Geodes

These are spherical to subspherical rock structures with internal cavities lined with mineral material. They have a durable exterior that resists more weather than the surrounding bedrock. It helps the geode survive intact as the surrounding bedrock wears away. The minerals lining the cavity are usually glowing clumps of tiny quartz crystals supported by multiple translucent gray and white agate bands. Many are full of more spectacular treasures.

Rich purple amethyst, flawless white calcite crystals, and colored banded agate are part of the common coating. Rare geodes can be filled with beautiful gems of blue silica, pink rhodochrosite, spectacular opals with vibrant colors, or other rare materials. Geodes come in many sizes, from less than a centimeter to several meters, which is the dream of those we seek, that we find one of those. From the outside, most geodes look like ordinary rocks, but when you open them, the views are breathtaking.

It's Love at First Sight

Most geologists love geodes. However, it is quite common for the public to melt by them. They were delighted and surprised that an uninteresting rock could contain a beautiful group of gemstone crystals, a layer of agate with colored bands, or both in the same cavity. Every year, people who have never taken a geology class buy thousands of tons of geodes, which are opened, sawn, and polished. They buy them because they love them. They love tiny lenses as jewelry, serrated and polished lenses as bookends, and spectacular amethyst lenses as home or office décor.

Around the world, geode locations have created revenue streams for those who collect them, prepare them for markets, and ship them to places purchased as objects of science, natural art, and enjoyment. Brazil, Uruguay, Mexico, and Namibia are four examples of geodesy becoming a local industry.

Geodes are soon sold at gem and mineral exhibits, museums, specialty stores, art galleries, and sites selling international or natural gifts. When geode opening demonstrations are held at the Rock and Mineral Show, they always draw crowds, and when a good geode is opened, the crowd usually produces enthusiastic cheers and gasps. There is something special about this beautiful treasure hidden in a rock that looks absolutely normal from the outside.

The Location of the Geodes

Geodes are not everywhere. Instead, they are usually abundant in regions where rocks form in unique geochemical environments. Most geode sites are located in A) layered volcanic deposits, such as basalt and tuff, or B) layered carbonate deposits, such as limestone and dolomite. Several other environments produce small amounts of geodesics.

Geodes are formed in many different ways, and there are several valid theories about their formation. This section does not provide the various ways a single or full-coverage ground cable can be formed.

VOLCANIC GEODES

The most famous and sought-after is that form in areas of volcanic activity. Voids in basalt lava flows are often filled with agate, quartz, opal, and other materials from hydrothermal vents or groundwater. Some voids are spaces occupied by gases that fail to escape the lava flow before forming a crust on their surface.

Where does all the gas come from? Some magmas contain large amounts of dissolved gases. It can be gas dissolved in several percentages by weight. (Think about it: the percentage by weight of gas!) As this magma rises to the surface, the gas expands as the pressure decreases. When magma erupts as a lava flow, so much gas is released that not everything can escape. When lava solidifies, some of that gas gets trapped in the lava, creating a large cavity.

Other voids in solidified lava flows occur when liquid lava flows flow after only partially solidifying. These small "lava tubes" generate incredible, large, and longest geodes. Many cathedral geodes are offshoots of these lava tubes, which were then filled with mineral materials. Many of them have the geometry of long branches, almost a meter in diameter and several meters long.

SEDIMENTARY GEODES

Geodesics in sedimentary rocks are commonly found in limestone, dolomite, and calcareous shale. In these reservoirs, gas-filled voids can serve as openings for geode formation. Shells, branches, roots, and other organic matter often decompose, leaving gaps for the mineral matter to form. These cavities can be filled with quartz, opal, agate, or carbonate minerals. They are usually smaller than geodes formed in volcanic rocks.

Geodes are easier to collect when your host rock is worn. It happens because basalt, limestone, dolomite, and shale are weathered more easily and quickly than the quartz and chalcedony that normally form the geode layer. The host rock erodes, and the geodes remain on the surface, washed away by currents or stranded on the remaining soil. In these cases, it is easy to find and collect geodesics. Some geodes are created by extracting the bedrock, but this method is difficult, expensive, and often damages the geodes.

The Names of the Geodes

Geodes have several names. The word "geode" usually has before the name of the mineral material that fills the geode. "Agate geode" and "Amethyst geode" are examples. The word "geode" can also be preceded by a geographical or stratigraphic name. "Keokuk Geode" and "Brazilian Geode" are examples.

Geode Marketing

An unopened geode looks like an uninteresting rock. They become even more interesting when they are opened, and their internal crystals and bands of agate become visible. While every crystal-clad geode is a miracle of nature, many things can make it a more marketable product and increase its value.

Products Can Be Made

Large agate geodes are usually cut into flat-bottomed blocks to make cute bookends, stationery sets, watch faces, or paperweights. Those onyx gray, white, or other less interesting colors are usually dyed bright blue, purple, green, red, or other colors and then polished to make them more attractive. These treatments allow bookends to sell faster and increase in value beyond the price paid for less interesting grays.

In decoration, it is also used:

Large amethyst-coated geodes are often expertly cut to reveal the amethyst crystals inside. They are then sawn and weighed as a support to be used as home or office décor items.

Portions of agate-clad lava tube earth are often used to create "cathedral lands" several feet high. These were cut in a way that exposed the amethyst-lined cavity very well, then sawn into a flat base, filled with metal-weighted concrete to make the geode stand upright, and the edges of the cavity were sanded to achieve a good finish. The Exterior and exterior are painted to hide scratches and wear during picking and shipping. Many of these large geodes cost thousands of dollars each.

Small geodes are often cut and polished. Beautiful slices can be displayed "as is" on a specially-made frame or support. Some of the sheer beauty is displayed in stained glass windows or panels. Less spectacular specimens can be dyed and used to make wind chimes, coasters, or decorative magnets. Small lenses with attractively colored lenses are often cut into small pieces that can be placed upright or used as flat plates to display items.

To open a geode, you need to have the tools so:

Kits to Open a Geode

Small, thin-walled geodes are usually available in kits at departmental, educational, scientific, travel, and novelty stores. The seller's product description encourages teachers, parents, and students to purchase the kit and break the geode with a hammer. These geode kits are very popular. If you Google "geode kit," you'll find them online from dozens of providers.

If you are considering buying one of these kits, check the reviews beforehand, as the quality is very variable. It is also important to plan the proper safety equipment since hitting the geodesic indicator with a hammer can cause rock fragments to fly and cause serious injuries, put on the equipment I recommended earlier. You also need a good place to do this activity. On the advice of some providers, breaking them on desks or classroom floors can lead to property damage and costly repairs.

Another way to buy a "pocket kit" every year is to buy some sample droppings and cut pockets. It can be supplemented with computer projection to view geodes on the website and videos of professionals opening geodes on YouTube. These avoid safety issues, property damage, and cleanup of "destroyed geodes." The cost of this approach can save money over time for other fun science activities.

Geodes Without Crystals

Everyone wants to find geometric crystals full of brightness when opening geodes. But sometimes there are other interesting landscapes in the interior. When there are no geometric crystals, one of the most common discoveries is a geode coated with chalcedony, quartz crystallite.

Chalcedony crystals are extremely small that cannot be seen with the naked eye. In the geode, a tiny chalcedony crystal sticks to the wall and is coated with tiny chalcedony crystals that point outward from the seed. One layer after another is placed, and in the end, it is a small hemisphere adhered and generated one on another, leaving a landscape that looks like grapes in clusters. This hemispherical geometry is a common crystalline chalcedony habit called grape-shaped.

Fake Geodes

Like most popular or valuable products, people have made fake "geodes" and sold them as items naturally. If you're a collector of spectacular geodes at premium prices, you'll need to know enough about them and their mineral materials to spot fakes. Expert gemologists, mineral collectors, paleontologists, and others who buy expensive specimens are often fooled by fakes.

Geodes, Nodules, Vugs, Concretions, and Thundereggs

Geodes, nodules, veins, and lightning are places on Earth where material dissolved in groundwater settles to form crystals or round objects. These objects have many characteristics and are formed through processes that resemble each other. In addition, both generate objects that attract attention and stimulate discussion. These objects are often confused with each other, and their names are used incorrectly because the speaker misinterprets the word or misinterprets the object. People in different parts of the world also use them differently. Who is right, and who is not? Here are some generalizations drawn from the common uses of these words.

Geodes have a hollow space inside or once had a hollow space filled with precipitation mineral material. The precipitated mineral material fills the cavity mainly by concentric internal growth. They have a competent outer coating that separates them from the host rock. This qualified outer coating allows many geodes to fracture and survive the complete disintegration of the host rock due to weathering. Geodes can then be taken from the earth's surface, dug into the ground, or found in riverbeds.

Nodules are solid pieces that are composed of precipitated mineral material. Maybe they have been hollow (and a geode) at one point and then filled with precipitated mineral material. They may also have formed through the growth of minerals on the surface of sediments, growth within cavities, or replacing their host rock.

Vugs are cavities that may contain crystals but do not have an effective coating capable of separating them from the bedrock. Unlike many geodes, they can cease to exist after the host rock has worn away.

Concretions are solid aggregates composed of deposited particles and cementitious material. They form when chemical precipitation begins around cores in sediments such as fossil grains or minerals. As more and more material accumulates around the Earth's core, nodules grow in three dimensions, filling pore spaces and displacing mineral grains. Their growth begins in the center and expands outward without a cavity while geodes grow from a cavity with minerals growing inward.

Thundereggs are spherical to subspherical rhyolite blocks eroded by volcanic formations. They have an internal cavity filled with agate, opal, or other mineral materials. Thundereggs rarely contain mineral crystals that grow in a vacuum.

Geode Localities in the United States

Some regions of the United States are known for their lenses and lens-like objects. Geodes are so popular in some states that they have earned the status of "Official National Rocks" or "Official National Gems." The Iowa State Legislature designated the Quartz Geode as the official "State Rock" in 1967; the Oregon Senate designated Thunderegg as the official "state rock" in 1965. The Minnesota State Legislature designated Lake Superior as an official state jewel in 1969. Some of the most notable locations are described below. There are many more, and a good place to read some of them is a book by Brad L. Cross and June Culp Zeitner called Geodes: Nature's Treasures.

KEOKUK GEODES

One of the most famous geodes in the world is the area around the community of Keokuk in Iowa. It is located near the confluence of the three states of Illinois, Iowa, and Missouri, and the geodes of the region are located in three states. Geodes were formed in the limestone and dolomite of the Mississippi-era Warsaw Formation. Most of these geodes are a few centimeters wide, with an outer layer of chalcedony from white to gray to bluish-gray and an interior lined with tiny quartz crystals. Most geodes have broken off their original carbonate rocks and are now found in local soils and river sediments. Some geodes contain interesting crystals of ankerite, aragonite, calcite, dolomite, goethite, gypsum, kaolinite, marcasite, millerite, pyrite, sphalerite, and other minerals. Some were found to have liquid oil in them.

LAKE SUPERIOR AGATE

Lake Superior Agate is a fortified agate that fills cavities in basalt flows formed in the Lake Superior region more than a billion years ago. Over time, silica-rich groundwater filled these cavities with agate and crystalline quartz. Most of them are filled and are more correctly called "nodules." However, some still retain cavities usually lined with crystalline quartz. Agates are usually reddish-brown, red, and orange-red. Traces of iron incorporated into agate cause these colors. Today, they are found on beaches, streams, agricultural soils, and glaciers.

GEODES OF KENTUCKY

Parts of the Fort Payne and Warsaw-Salem formations in Kentucky contain numerous geodes. These have been eroded from their host rock units and are now found in the valleys of streams. Other areas where many geodes have been found in Kentucky creeks include the Green River and the former Kentucky River terraces in the south-central state.

WISCONSIN GEODES

The Wisconsin Natural and Geological History Service report a large presence of geodes, Lake Superior agate nodules, and thunder eggs in the state. These have been sold in Ashland, Chippewa, Clark, Crawford, Douglas, Dunn, Grant, La Crosse, Milwaukee, Pepin, Pierce, St. Croix, Sheboygan, Trempello, and Ward Sherbourne County.

DUGWAY GEODES

It is one of the most interesting geode sites in the United States and is located in Juab County, Utah. Between 32,000 and 14,000 years ago, Lake Bonneville occupied a significant portion of what we know today as western Utah. The action of waves along the lakeshore caused erosion in the rhyolite flows containing the geodes. Wave action and erosion released the rhyolite geodes and deposited them in lake sediments several miles away, now known as Dugway Geode Beds.

Today, many seek out Dugway's geodes because they are thrilled to find its centers covered in agate and crystals. But some Dugway geodes also contain another hidden surprise: the incorporation of a small amount of uranium into their chalcedony coating causes the geode coating to emit a spectacular lime-green fluorescence under ultraviolet light. They probably have many collectors of fluorescent minerals interested in collecting geodes.

INDIANA GEODES

Geodes are frequently seen in exhibits in the Harrodsburg Limestone and Ramp Creek formations in south-central Indiana. The Indiana Geological Survey reports that geodesy meters abound along the creek and stretch over several miles of land on either side of its upwelling area.

WOODBURY GEODES

Woodbury Geodes is located in the area near Woodbury, Tennessee. They originate from the limestone and dolomite of the Warsaw Formation and can be seen where these rocky units emerge. The released geodes were found in the residual soil above the rock units that formed them and in the sediments of the valleys that drained these areas. They are chalcedony-coated geodes with a quartz crystal interior.

ARIZONA GEM SILICA GEODES

Unusual geodes and nodules found at Inspiration Mine in Gila County, Arizona, are coated with silica gem, a rare, beautiful, valuable blue chalcedony. Some have discovered silica gem stalactites!

Oregon Thundereggs

Thundereggs are not geodes, but they are so similar that they are at least worth mentioning in this section. Oregon is the most famous Thunder Egg city in the world. Thundereggs have been found in rhyolite and tuff deposits in many parts of the state. In 1965, the Oregon Legislature passed a resolution making Thunderegg the state's official rock. The state has a mine egg museum and places to enter, pay a small fee, and search for mine eggs to take home.

Other Famous Sites

There are hundreds of regions on the planet where you can find geodesics of various types in abundance. Most of these reservoirs are small and support the gathering activities of a small number of hunting dogs. However, other deposits abound, and there is enough land to support commercial harvesting and manufacturing.

Oco (Eight) Geodes

The Oco or Ocho geodes are small and composed of agate coated with Druze quartz found in the Tres Pinheiros region of Brazil. They range in size from about 1/2 to 3 inches in diameter and are vesicles formed by basalt flows that lie beneath parts of the area. Most Oco geodes have a thin layer of agate, an open interior, and an inner cluster of tiny, sharp quartz tips about 1/8 inch long. When worn out, basalt flows form a reddish-brown soil, and crystals, which are more weatherproof than basalt, accumulate in the soil.

When the deposits were first mined, the land was easy to find and became a local enterprise for those who collected and sold it. Many Oco geodes are cut in half, polished, or sliced and polished. These are sold in rock shops and novelty stores for lovers of interesting rocks and crystals. Because the crust of many Ocos is so thin, they are often packaged and sold as "broken geodes" kits. It is a popular activity for elementary students studying minerals and crystals in science class.

Amethyst Tonsils From Brazil and Uruguay

Undoubtedly, the most spectacular geode deposits discovered are amethyst tonsil basalts from the Brazilian state of Rio Grande do Sul and neighboring Uruguay. About 160 million years ago, when the Atlantic Ocean opened up and plate tectonics separated Africa and South America, one of the world's largest basalt floods occurred. The basalt flows out of the crack, creating lava flows in layers thousands of feet thick.

In these flows, bubbles and lava tubes create cavities lined first with a layer of agate and then with a full layer of thick crystalline quartz. At this point, geodes are formed but filled with crystals instead of amethyst. However, because these geodes are still buried, they are illuminated by the decay of radioactive minerals in the surrounding basalt. This radiation creates color centers in quartz, turning transparent quartz into amethyst. The resulting geodes are beautiful, some large. Today, they are meticulously mined, sawn, and displayed as gemstone ornaments in homes, offices, and museums.

Some amethyst geodes are heated in a high-temperature furnace. This treatment causes the oxidation of iron which causes it to appear purple. The result is a color change from amethyst quartz to citrine quartz.

The Largest Geode in the World?

Geology.com has many articles on world records related to earth sciences. These include the highest tsunami, the largest volcano, the geyser, and more. We know from these records that choosing the largest, highest, deepest, etc., can lead to disagreements about measurement methods, scoring criteria, etc.

Similar questions revolve around the name of the "world's largest geode." The definition of a geodesic, measurement method, reliability of large geodetic reports, etc., choose the "maximum" problematic. So, let's point out a geode that we think fits the definition and has a pretty impressive size. Some researchers call it "the largest geode in the world," others disagree, but most agree that it's really big.

"Geode de Pulpi" is located near Almeria, Spain. It has a volume of about 11 cubic meters and a width of about 12 meters. It is found in the Triassic dolomite and presents a discontinuous sequence of minerals, starting from iron carbonates and barite, through lapis lazuli, and finally to an interior cavity in which giant crystals of gypsum (selenite) stand out. The gypsum crystals are colorless and transparent and are said to "look like ice cubes." The geode was discovered in 1999 when it was traversed through a canal at the Mina Rica silver mine.

Fossils

They are the organic remains of plants and animals found in sedimentary rock formations and can be used to determine their age. It is done through so-called index fossils because they only existed in a given geological era or period.

To be considered fossils, they must present the following requirements:

1. That they can be easily identified and distinguished from all other fossils.
2. That it has lived for a relatively short geological time.
3. That presents a wide geographical distribution.
4. It has lived in different sedimentary basins and is seen in different rock types.

Fossilization is a series of physical, chemical, and biological processes through which organisms with a "normal" fate will be preserved as fossils that decompose completely after death. It means the passage of the organism from the biosphere to the lithosphere

Fossil record: includes all recorded fossil discoveries and their occurrences in sedimentary rocks and fossils that have not yet been discovered and described.

Fossilization potential: this is an intrinsic characteristic in each organism and is likely to be preserved in the fossil record.

Trilobites

Trilobites are a group of fossil arthropods that lived in the Paleozoic, appeared in the Cambrian 542 million years ago, and became extinct at the end of the Permian before the arrival of the dinosaurs lived a total of about 300 million years; No other fauna can so clearly reflect the drama of the appearance, evolution and diversification and subsequent extinction. Among arthropods, they belong to the class Trilobites, divided into about 5,000 species in 8 orders, 150 families, and 1,400 genera.

They lived in ancient oceans, and their fossilized remains can be found today in the petrified sediments of these oceans on every continent. Humans first noticed them around 25,000 years ago in France, in the "Cave of the Trilobites," a Cro-Magnon man found one and made a hole in it to use as a pendant or amulet. Specimens with similar uses have appeared in Egypt, Greece, and Rome, and even in Asturias, recently appeared in the remains of three thin sheets of part of its exoskeleton.

Ammonites

Ammonites are a group of fossil animals of great importance in paleontology. The first representatives of this group appeared during the Devonian period, about 400 million years ago, and became extinct 65 million years ago in the Great Crisis that marked the end of the Cretaceous. During this long time, they underwent a rapid evolution of forms, many of which were widespread in the oceans of the time. As a result, the shells of these cephalopods can date rocks fairly accurately to large areas of the planet. So, it's no surprise that reference fossils were chosen to develop stratigraphic scales, which paleontologists use to measure past time and represent events in Earth's history and life.

Platystrophia Ponderosa

Platystrophia is an extinct brachiopod that lived in Asia, Europe, North America, and South America from the Ordovician to the Silurian period. It has a prominent groove and folds. It usually lives in sands and calcareous marine silts.

CHAPTER #8
HOW TO IDENTIFY ROCKS

In this chapter, I want to explain how you are going to begin to identify rocks; beyond those I named you or searching the internet for the characteristics, my plan is that being in the mountain or excavating where you are when you take it out you recognize what type of rock it is and place it in the classification as you have structured it.

Let's start with how elementary the types of rocks are:

Mineral

In the case of a mineral, it is solid with a specific chemical formula and possesses a crystalline structure.

Gemstone

It is a mineral, rock, or organic material used to make jewelry and other ornaments.

Mineraloid

A mineral-like substance with no igneous, sedimentary, or metamorphic crystal structure?

It could be argued that they fall into all three categories! It all depends on where they formed and how they got to Earth.

Identifying the Rock Map

Is the "rock" soft enough to flatten with two fingers?

If this happens to you, I regret to tell you that you are surely kneading a piece of excrement or, failing that, a little mud.

But if not, you have to question more things, although if you read this book from Hawaii, maybe basalt is what you are looking at.

If You Drop Vinegar on the Rock, Does It Bubble?

If so, chances are its LIMESTONE OR MARBLE, but if it doesn't, you can ask the most important question:

Does the rock have layers?

It is the most important question. Now we have to go slowly, little by little, to understand the rock better and identify it, which is the plan of this chapter.

If It Is

If yes, you should check if the rock has crystals or large particles:

If so, it is most likely METAMORPHIC. It could be gneiss, shale, or quartzite! But if not, you should check if your rock is sandy or smooth.

If it is sandy, the question is: Does it look like a bunch of pebbles cemented in the sand?

If so, it is most likely to be a conglomerate, but if not, it may be sandstone.

If you feel it soft, the question is: when you hit it with your fingernail, what sound do you hear?

If the sound is "TINK," it is Slate… if it is "TUNK," it is Shale.

In Case You Don't (the Rock Doesn't Have Layers)

Now the question is; does the rock have crystals or large particles?

If so, it's most likely granite.

If not, but it is glassy and black, it is most likely obsidian.

If your rock doesn't have crystals or large particles, but there are some small chunks, and one looks a bit like a fish scale, it is probably a fossilized poop! (COPROLITO)…

I leave you an example of how to identify a type of rock:

Identifying Igneous Rocks

IDENTIFY THE TYPE OF TEXTURE OF THE ROCK

Igneous rocks come in 7 different texture classes, each with its own unique characteristics.

Igneous pegmatite rocks have very large crystals, more than 1 cm in size. These are types of igneous rocks formed by slow cooling.

Remember, the longer the rock cools, the larger the crystals.

Igneous amphibolite rocks are interlocking crystals smaller than pegmatite crystals but can still be seen with the naked eye.

Porphyry igneous rocks have crystals of two different sizes. Usually, the largest crystals are located in areas of the smaller crystals.

Cryptocrystalline igneous rocks have a dense texture, and most crystals are too small to be seen with the naked eye. You will need to use a magnifying glass to observe the crystals in the cryptocrystalline rock.

Igneous rocks that form crystals quickly have the so-called vitreous texture. Obsidian is the only igneous vitreous rock identified by its dark color. It looks like a dark black crystal.

Blister-shaped igneous rocks, such as pumice, appear to have bubbles and form before gas escapes, and lava forms rocks. It is also formed by very rapid cooling.

The texture of pyroclastic igneous rocks consists of very fine (ash) to very thick (tuff and gap) volcanic fragments.

LOOK AT THE COMPOSITION OF YOUR ROCK

Composition refers to the percentage of certain minerals in a rock. You will need a rock guide to determine what minerals are in your rock. There are four main types of igneous rock constituents.

If you are not a rock collector or an experienced geologist, identifying the composition of rocks can be very difficult.

If you have questions about identifying rocks, contact a collector or geologist at your local college or university.

Igneous felsic rocks are lighter in color. Its mineral components are mainly silicates such as feldspar and quartz.

Granite is an example of a felsic rock.

Felsic rocks are low-density and contain 0 to 15% mafic crystals. The mafic minerals are olivine, pyroxene, amphibole, and biotite.

Mafic igneous rocks are dark in color and mainly composed of magnesium and iron. They contain 46% to 85% mafic mineral crystals and have a high density.

Basalt is an example of a mafic rock.

Ultramafic igneous rocks are also darker in color and contain more mafic minerals. These rocks contain more than 85% mafic mineral crystals.

Dunite is an example of an ultramafic rock.

Intermediate igneous rocks contain 15% to 45% mafic mineral crystals. These share minerals with felsic and mafic rocks and are medium in color.

Diorite is an example of an intermediate rock.

LOOK AT YOUR ROCK LAYERS

The presence and distribution of layers can help you identify the main types of rocks you have.

If a rock has layers, it will have different sections of various colors and may or may not contain fossils or small crystals. You will have to look for them with a magnifying glass.

In a cross-section, the rock layers look like stripes of different colors stacked on each other.

The presence and distribution of layers can help you identify the main types of rocks you have.

Igneous rock has no layers. If your rock has layers, then it is metamorphic or sedimentary.

Sedimentary rocks have soft, brittle mud, sand, or gravel layers.

Sedimentary rocks can also have crystals. If the layers of your rock are made up of crystals of different sizes, then your rock is sedimentary.

Metamorphic rocks have layers composed of crystals of the same size.

Metamorphic rock formations also fold and deform.

CHECK YOUR ROCK FOR VISIBLE PARTICLES

You'll need to use a magnifying glass, as some particles and crystals may be so small that you won't see them with the naked eye. If your rock has visible grains, proceed to the next step to sort the rocks by grain type. If there are no visible particles, use the following criteria to classify rocks.

Igneous rocks are very dense and hard. These may have a glassy appearance.

Metamorphic rocks may also have a vitreous appearance. You can distinguish metamorphic rocks from igneous rocks because they are brittle, light in color, and dark black.

Sedimentary rocks without grains resemble dry mud or clay.

Sedimentary rocks without grains are soft and often easily scratched with a fingernail. These rocks also react with hydrochloric acid.

CHAPTER #9
TIPS YOU CAN USE TO FIND ROCKS

These tips come from expert hands, from someone immersed in the search for rocks who knows how to make life easier and find rocks faster. I hope you put them into practice.

If you are looking for jasper and semi-precious gemstones, I give you a tip, if you are looking for them in rivers, remember:

Rocks of the same density and specific gravity/weight will tend to increase speed in the same area or location.

Some common tips are:

Look for the Glow

When searching, you should pay attention to the intense colors, allowing you to recognize fake rocks from real ones.

Look for sharp edges.

Look for refractions and flashes.

Pay attention to brightness and texture.

Move the Rocks

Keep looking while you choose because your focus and your emotion rise on a stone that you are scrutinizing, but at the same time, you are missing what you find at a distance of a few centimeters.

Rest Your Eyes for a While

That's very important because our eyesight should always be rested so we can see more efficiently.

Another Very Important Tip if You Do Not Understand if You Have Found Brown Jasper or Flint

So, a lot of times when you're in the field and the rock is dirty, a trick you can use to determine if it's jasper or flint or in that family of rocks is to hit it against a rock known as basalt and if you hear it sound like glassy when you hit it, then you probably have chert or maybe flint.

So, You Can Get Rocks on the Banks of Rivers, Lakes, or Streams

When looking near or in a small stream, dip your hand, lift the stones and pebbles, take a quick look, and then (for added safety) dip your hand back a bit in the water to wet the stones; to do another check once they are brought to the surface (water will clean them slightly and rotate them, rotate, and change position in hand to see them from various angles).

If you are a beginner, it will be useful to know the various tips and improvements for this hobby. It's always good to learn something new.

The most important tip for rock hunting is to keep yourself and everyone around you safe. Then you need to know where you will look for rocks and determine if you need permission to look for rocks. Also, don't forget to bring enough equipment, so others know where you'll find rocks.

Tips to Remember When Doing Rockhounding

Rockhounding can soon move from an incredible hobby to a high-risk workspace. Your ability to keep yourself safe is based on taking your time while digging and knowing the tools you use to track rock.

While these tips may not cover all the tips for maintaining a safe rock hunt, hopefully, they will inspire you to make your own rules to follow.

Maybe you want to set a rule for yourself to come home when the sun starts to set. Either way, these tips will help you make the best decisions.

Know Your Route

You should always know where you are. In addition to knowing where you are, try to research what harmful plants or wildlife are in the area.

You want to master as many aspects of the route as possible. It allows you to plan and pack better.

Know Your Mission

Do you know what minerals you're looking for, or are you going to explore them on the go? Figure out how you want to spend your time searching for rocks because that will put you in the right mindset.

The Right Checklist

If you feel like you tend to forget something, create a list of the tools you're going to need. If you're looking for a particular rock, you may need tools other than what you're used to. With a checklist, you won't lose or forget anything.

Appropriate Clothing

The right clothes you have, like the ones I addressed chapters ago, will make your rock exploration time even better. Wearing sandals while walking on a trail or creek won't make you a happy camper. A breathable shirt and gloves protect your hands as well as other implements.

Have Technology

You must have the right power and skill when you extract these minerals.

You don't want to hit a rock too hard and accidentally eject it. Precise use of tools for different needs.

Protect Your Eyes

Wear glasses no matter how soft the stone is. Any fragment that flies while hammering can become lodged in your eyes. And how it hurts!

Protect Your Tools

When we find something, we can start letting it go. Perhaps there's a stronger stone on top of the one you're trying to restore? Do not use these tools differently than they were designed for your use. You can damage them faster and injure yourself.

Care

Be careful if you're in an area with falling rocks or stones or just sitting on top of you. Try wearing a helmet if you think something hard will hit your head.

If you have children, ensure they are as protected as you are. Teach them the importance of taking the initiative and listening to your instructions. Show them how to handle the tools to avoid unnecessary mistakes.

Rockhounding is a hobby many enjoy alone or with a group of people. Join the rock treasure hunt, which creates great connections with other people who know your love of geology. Also, if something were to happen to you, your group members would be there to help you.

However, if you're new to Rockhounding, there are a few suggestions to follow. These tips will allow you to learn, have fun and minimize the risk of dangerous situations.

- **Never go looking for rocks alone.** My advice is to go with someone more informed than you so that you have teachers and leaders.
- **Do not seek to dive into the most hidden caves or the riskiest cliffs.** Start by sticking to basic beginner areas to learn with minimal risk.
- **Do your research.** You don't want to search for rocks blindly because you may never find anything. Any person wants to know where to go and what materials to find there.
- **Don't get upset with radioactive material until you have experience.** It can lead to serious health problems if you don't know what you're doing.
- **Only take what you can reasonably use.** It allows others to enjoy the area without the material.
- **If you choose to travel, stop at the nearest city and ask where you're going.** Be as prepared as possible.
- **Don't be afraid to ask those "silly" questions.** When it comes to safety if it keeps you alive and out of harm's way, it's unquestionably stupid.

Any advice that comes from common sense and that you feel puts your life at risk, keep it in mind because the plan is that you return with beautiful rocks and not that you suffer a setback.

CHAPTER #10
HOW TO CLEAN YOUR ROCKS

What a great joy when you find rocks in the ground and protect them in your things and then study them at home, but you have to check calmly and clean them so that you do not scratch or hit them, so in this chapter, I will leave you a series of tips for you to do the cleaning successfully.

This chapter is dedicated to those advanced beginners who have decided to immerse themselves in this wonderful world.

A Tip That Few People Know

Cut a lemon in half, squeeze on the stone, then leave the two halves of the lemon on the stone and rest on it for 24 hours. The next day you will see a big difference. After this step, you can go to the next step, place your rocks on a tray with citric acid inside.

Why should you use lemons?

Because they are one of the highest in alkalines! And are super high in acid on the pH scale.

Other Tips for Cleaning

You can use lemon juice to clean rocks (your agates, for example) with peroxide and CLR.

If you have unwanted calcite, you can use white vinegar to dissolve it.

Another more important point is: the citric acid crystals you used must be resolved in "hot water," or they can simply crystallize and not do their job.

Another tip for removing agate rust stains due to iron content is to use something called

Rust Out, let them soak for 24 hours (maybe longer), and brush them with a toothbrush. No damage agate.

You can also use a powdered sink cleaner with oxalic acid as an ingredient, as it will be much milder than a heavy solution of pure oxalic acid.

Use baking soda to neutralize the acid of lemons or any acid; this way, the solution will not continue in its oxidation process when you empty it.

A Diamond Tips

Here's a truly precious and rare tip: after rinsing your rocks thoroughly, you can dry them and soak them in "mineral oil" that fills the inclusions, and then you can clean up the excess. You let it soak for days or weeks and then remove it and put it on a plate (covered with paper towels to absorb the extra oil), but you'll still have to clean each one until the excess oil is removed. After this process, they will look almost polished. They will look great (for example, on heavy glass, glass plates, or bowls with small LED lights). They're going to be great.

Watch Out for These Safety Tips

Be careful when mixing different acids and solutions, sulfuric acid could be created, and you should not breathe it. It is harmful.

Use old plastic containers with lids.

PLEASE DO NOT ADD BLEACH TO THE MIXTURE! It will cause chlorine gas which can kill you.

In a practical way and following my advice, you will see how to clean your beautiful rocks.

CHAPTER #11
HOW TO CUT YOUR ROCKS

The raw mineral usually has a bland appearance, and few find it interesting, even though its natural beauty is already attractive. That is why some minerals are always given different treatments and shapes according to the hardness and composition of each one through cutting, polishing, and laminating processes using special machines and tools.

The most striking and highest-quality gemstones are those commonly used in mineral jewelry. In the process of cutting and polishing gemstones for jewelry (called desertification), the physical and optical properties of the gemstone, such as hardness and cleavage, should be considered. The stone removal process involves cutting the gemstone with a saw or diamond disc cutter, starting with a grinder, and finally carving and polishing it until it is smooth and shiny.

Gemstones are often cut into cabochons or facets for optical and color effects. The cabochons are cut so that one side is round and the other flat. In the case of moonstone and labradorite, cabochon allows you to appreciate the reflections of color better. In the case of transparent gemstones, the most commonly used cut is faceting, carving the surface into several flat surfaces to enhance the beauty and brilliance of the gemstone.

I will leave you a series of tips on cutting and polishing precious stones, information you will not find anywhere else.

All rockhounds have always wondered if there is a perfect way to cut their rocks. Obviously, the answer does not exist, but many variables exist. Certainly, there are actions/ways that work better, and others work worse.

If You Don't Have Tools to Cut Your Rocks

You can go to a "Lapidary." Find a Lapidary Club near where you are. You can join your club and cut the rock using the club's equipment. It's all going to depend on what you have.

Many times, they will make cuts for you for a minimal fee. So do your research and talk to colleagues so they can give you related information, and they'll even do you the favor of cutting it off or telling you how to do it.

If You Want to Cut the Stones but Don't Have a Saw

You can use a lapidary saw or file, but it depends on what we have to cut.

First, you must stabilize the stone in a watering can, install a non-slip mat, and naturally grab the stone between your fingers.

Dip the stone in the water with your hands and start with a half-round row that has a narrow edge.

Keep the stone moist so as not to burn and contain its properties and appearance.

If the crack in your cut begins to turn white (or the color of the stone begins to change), then it's time to use a toothbrush to clean the crack, restore the color of the stone, then rinse it with water and follow with your cut.

If you want to cut your rocks with a saw, then you should know the following information.

You will come across 3 basic types of saws regarding rocks. All of them will use oil or water to lubricate the blade:

- Tile saws.
- Cutting saws (basically, just a wet table saw for rocks).
- Slab saw.

Before you start, you should consider how big and hard your rocks are to choose the right saw. I think you should also consider how expert/advanced you are.

You can also use a manual grinder with a stone-cutting blade.

If You Have a Tile Saw

To begin, I leave you some advantages:

- They are cheaper and easier to find.
- It's a good way to do it, but it doesn't allow you to cut very large rocks.
- For hard and large stones, if you don't want to spend thousands on the saw and more for oil, blades, and maintenance, you can use the oil slab saws in your club (or lapidary society).

A more important question to ask to cut your stones is: Which blade should I use?

- You must have a tile saw with a diamond edge blade.
- You can also use a cutting saw with a diamond blade or a grinder with a diamond blade.
- Stones cut with a diamond blade work quite well because, for example, if your cut is for agate material, you will probably want a diamond sheet in it.
- Any saw you have; you must have diamond blades on all saws.

Another important question is:

How Many Inches Should the Blade Have?

For a correct answer, you should ask another question: how big is your rock?

Wet saw with a 7 or 8-inch blade, but ideal for smaller things.

Remember, the advice is: buy the tile saw as big as possible. You can cut smaller rocks with a large saw, but you can't cut bigger rocks with a smaller saw.

In the end, we can see that a tile saw with a diamond blade of up to 10 inches is a good starting point for beginners, but for example, the cuts will not be as fine or as smooth, also cutting with mineral oil and inverting the pulleys so that the blade rotates faster so that you can cut by hand very quickly.

Tile saws are also harder to get smooth, straight cuts if you're holding the stones in your hand and therefore require a lot of practice.

So, if you're crazy about rockhounding and stones in general and are on a budget, you should buy an oiled slab saw.

I advise you to buy that if you have an organized place to cut your rocks (for example, your garage)

Why Is an Oil Slab Saw the Best Professional Choice?

They are the best and safest tools, but they are expensive.

However, the blades will last much longer than cutting hard rocks like jasper and agates with water in a tile saw.

These are the ones with covers and vice that feed the rock through the saw, either by weight or motor.

If you cut your stones in a lapidary society, you will usually find and use an oiled slab saw.

Safety Tips

- Use the right safety equipment and tools.
- Wear eye protection and a good mask.
- Put the rock in some space to prevent injury to it.
- Always use a diamond blade. When cutting rock, the types of blades you deal with are generally much safer than the blades you see used for wood or other things. You can touch the edge of the spinning saw with a bare finger and not hurt yourself because the continuous-edge diamond blades will not cut you. Segmented diamond blades will take your fingers and never slow down.

Other Tips

If you have to cut a few beads, a rotating tool can often be too messy.

What if I want to make holes in crystals for pendants? What type of bit should it be used for? A drill bit impregnated with diamond.

Curiosities to Know About How to Cut and What Results You Can Have

If you're cutting a rough rock with gaps, the orientation of the cut doesn't matter. Its result could be a colorful mix of small gravel rocks.

If you are cutting a mountain agate rock, the orientation of the cut should be through the area with reddish agate. Your result could be a mixture of clear and red/orange.

If you cut an unidentified rock find, the cutting orientation should be through the band-like area. Your result: I don't know. Agate band designs?

Remember: Some rocks don't need to be cut. Just a Pole, and they are good!

CHAPTER #12
HOW TO POLISH YOUR ROCKS

Rock polishing is a hobby that produces beautiful results. It can be done with the minimum necessary equipment or by purchasing a polishing drum that can process several rocks simultaneously.

For rock collectors, learning how to polish them to reveal their natural beauty is just as important as the collection itself. Polishing rock does not require any extraordinary skill. It just requires patience and interest. The following steps will help you keep your collection in tip-top shape. Best of all, the tools we will need are relatively inexpensive, and we will achieve a spectacular finish.

We have collected our stones, and perhaps we have also cut them. But now, what do we do with them?

If we want to use them to decorate our spaces, we may need to polish them.

How can we polish our stones?

I leave you a series of tips of great value:

The first case is if you don't have time to spend hours making the rocks shine:

You can spray them with polyurethane; some people call it cheating. Ok, but you don't have time!

The only negative is that exposure to the climate will have dew that will come off, and not in the best way.

You can also use the following:

- Polishing discs.
- You can send it to get the shine you want.

Here's a Secret No One Knows

You can rub baby oil on the rocks to polish them.

You can also use a car polisher with diamond grains if you have one.

Polishing gemstones with a 15-pound glass (Thumler's) is another option; if you want to do that, then you need some tips:

Do not combine different types of stones because the stones have very different hardness levels.

If you have corundum-like rubies, you will wear out softer stones badly, while rubies will have a lower level of polishing.

For final polishing, harder stones will continue to scratch softer stones, and polishing will not be consistent.

Another secret:

At the end of the polishing process, you can use "ivory soap" It has great results!

A Step-by-Step to Polish the Stones

Cleaning

Clean the stone well with soap and water without leaving sand or other materials that hinder our work.

Shaping

If you want to give a special shape to the stone, you can use a chisel with a hammer to make the desired finish. Do not forget to wear protective glasses to avoid accidents.

Use 80-Grain Sandpaper

After wetting the rock, sand it with lower-grained sandpaper (80). Start sanding the rock with a constant rotational motion. When using sandpaper, keep soaking the rock in the water. Continue sanding the rock until it is the desired shape and size. This process should continue until the rock reaches the desired smoothness.

Use 180-Grain Sandpaper

Wet the rock again and sand it with 180-grain paper to remove the deeper scratches below the surface.

Use 600-Grain Sandpaper

Wet the rock again and sand it with 600-grain sandpaper to further soften it and remove the slightest scratches. Continue to immerse the rock in the water to remove dust.

Mineral Polishing Comes

Wet and remove excess moisture with thick fabrics such as denim. Put a small amount of polisher on a damp cloth and use it to polish the rock with small circles around it.

Continue dipping the cloth in the enamel and polishing the rock until you get the desired result. You can do this process manually or use a Dremel to help you manually reach complex areas.

CONCLUSION

If you reached the end, I congratulate you and thank you for having traveled this wonderful path of looking for rocks like a professional. Remember that I prepared this book with dedication and experience so that you go from a beginner to an advanced one and get optimal results.

I hope you leave me a positive review after reading the knowledge I shared here.

"I encourage you to publish a photo of the rocks found after cleaning or polishing them with the advice I left you".

Rockhounding: A hobby shared by amateur geologists who collect and search for natural rocks and minerals to study and enjoy. It's a hobby that anyone can explore simply in their backyard and then expand to nearby areas and beyond.

To begin, you will require some tools: as I explained in their respective chapter, a rock hammer, a magnifying glass, a notebook, protective glasses, geological references, a sample bag, and a backpack.

The most important thing is information about where you can safely and legally look and where you can't.

You can collect on private land if you have the owner's consent. Logging along major roads is prohibited and generally unsafe. Off the beaten track is fine, but always watch for vehicles and wear brightly colored clothes.

Public lands, as you can see, have a series of restrictions to preserve our natural resources. That is why removing rocks and minerals are prohibited and with great regulations.

All rocks and sediments are composed of minerals, and for example, Maryland has more than 100 separate units of rocks and sediments. Its type will mainly determine the class of minerals that can be found in it, but other factors, such as groundwater that are rich in minerals, cracks, fissures, and voids in the rock, and the chemical composition of the overlying rock units can also affect whether minerals are formed.

Quartz, mica, and feldspar are the best known. Less common minerals include calcite, garnet, tourmaline, siderite, pyrite, hematite, limonite, and amphibole. These are very small, almost microscopic minerals and may not be seen as examples of crystals in books, but they are there.

Happy search, my dear rockhounder!

Made in the USA
Las Vegas, NV
20 November 2023

81214246R00063